Mature Friendships, Love, and Romance

Mature Friendships, Love, and Romance

A Practical Guide to Intimacy for Older Adults

MORLEY D. GLICKEN

 PRAEGER

AN IMPRINT OF ABC-CLIO, LLC
Santa Barbara, California • Denver, Colorado • Oxford, England

Library of Congress Cataloging-in-Publication Data

Glicken, Morley D.
   Mature friendships, love, and romance : a practical guide to intimacy for older adults / Morley D. Glicken.
      p. cm.
   Includes bibliographical references and index.
   ISBN 978–0–313–38242–0 (hbk. : alk. paper) — ISBN 978–0–313–38243–7 (ebook)
1. Love in old age. 2. Older people—Psychology. 3. Intimacy (Psychology)
I. Title.
HQ1061.G583   2010
155.67—dc22   2010000165

ISBN: 978–0–313–38242–0
EISBN: 978–0–313–38243–7

14 13 12 11 10   1 2 3 4 5

This book is also available on the World Wide Web as an eBook.
Visit www.abc-clio.com for details.

Praeger
An Imprint of ABC-CLIO, LLC

ABC-CLIO, LLC
130 Cremona Drive, P.O. Box 1911
Santa Barbara, California 93116-1911

This book is printed on acid-free paper (∞)

Manufactured in the United States of America

Portions of this text were published in *Evidence-Based Counseling and Psychotherapy for an Aging Population*, by Morley D. Glicken, pages 132–134, 361–362, and 377–379. Copyright Elsevier (2009).

This book is dedicated to my parents, Sam and Rose Glicken,
who were loving and tender with one another and
with their children, through good and bad times,
and who modeled mature love in everyway imaginable

Contents

Preface

This is a book for older adults who want to resolve issues of intimacy, romance, and friendships and develop positive relationships with their children and family members. It is a serious book because the subject is a serious one. Love is life-sustaining. Romance is just as vital to older people as it to younger people, and loneliness, as we age without good friends and positive relationships with our families and children, is everything it's cracked up to be.

As I began researching what others had written about older adult relationships, I found that almost all of it was about sex. The few books I found on relationships with family and children were often full of psychobabble and silly advice. How serious can books be with titles like *The Juicy Tomatoes Guide to Ripe Living After 50*; *How Not to Become a Little Old Lady*; *Juicy Tomatoes: Plain Truths, Dumb Lies, and Sisterly Advice About Life After 50*; *Better Than I Ever Expected: Straight Talk About Sex After Sixty*, and I could go on.

I'm 69 and I think I know something about every aspect of what this book will cover from my own life experiences. I've also been a social work practitioner working with older adults and a professor of social work training graduate students to work with older adults. From these experiences I can tell you that relationships are tremendously important to people as we age. As a result, I promise I won't approach the need for healthy and life-enhancing relationships in a frivolous way.

I hope you will find this book to be a wealth of information, easily written, and filled with stories from older adults about their relationships, good and bad. The stories come from real older people who have something to say. I've asked them to write honestly about themselves and not to give pat answers to tough life problems. You will find some of the stories very moving with positive outcomes, and others touching, but hurtful. I want you to experience a range of stories. Perhaps you will find a story that is close to the issues you're dealing with and it will help you resolve some of your relationship problems—or if not resolve them, at least understand them better.

Men are as concerned about relationships as women, but from the wealth of books written for older adult women you wouldn't think men exist or have concerns about their relationships with others. They do and I've tried, in the stories written by men and the research I've presented, to make this book relevant to men and to women.

I believe that the last third of our lives can be our best years. The people who come into our lives have potential to be the very truest friends we'll ever have. The people we love deeply can add happy and productive years to our lives. In writing this book, I'm also aware that many of us have troubled and hurtful relationships with others, and I promise to write this book mindful of Bertrand Russell's words that we should all have "unbearable sympathy for the suffering of others," particularly those of us who write books to help others.

Dr. Morley D. Glicken
Prescott, Arizona

Acknowledgments

I want to thank my editor at Praeger/ABC-CLIO, Debbie Carvalko, for taking my idea about a book on mature love and letting me run with it. It's a topic near and dear to my mature heart and Praeger/ABC-CLIO gives its authors a great deal of freedom to develop ideas in the most creative ways a writer can imagine, so many thanks to Debbie and to my publisher.

Because this book used a number of personal stories about mature love, and since the authors asked for anonymity, I want to thank all of them for sharing such touching and powerful work. None of the authors are professional writers but I think you will feel, as I do, that their stories touch our hearts and move us. Thank you, my friends and colleagues, for contributing your stories to this book.

I have friends and loved ones who model mature love in many important ways. My new friend and tennis partner, Barry Kravitz, is a wonderful example of mature friendship. In a recent e-mail, he wrote, "When I moved away from Santa Barbara, I felt I left five 'brothers' behind who were part of the men's group I belonged to. It was gut-wrenching to move and to alter the 'brotherhood.' However, I really feel a brotherly companionship with you—and I thank you for being who you are." Thank you, Barry, for giving me such a true and meaningful example of mature friendship.

My sister Gladys Smith and I have a mature relationship that grows better every day. Her example gave me a model for writing about the mature relationships between family members.

I couldn't have written about children without the example of my daughter, Amy Glicken, who is a gift to an aging father and who contributed some wonderful stories to this and other books I've written.

Finally, to those people in my life who have being loving partners and whose model of relationships encouraged me to share my vision of mature love, the best advice I ever got came from John Lennon who said, loving isn't about never having to say you're sorry . . . it's about saying you're sorry every five minutes . . . and meaning it.

CHAPTER 1

Love, Intimacy, Family, and Friendships in a Time of Ageism

INTRODUCTION

We live in a time when growing numbers of older adults enjoy good health, financial independence, and the ability to pursue a long and happy life. And yet, when it comes to older love and intimacy, many people think that these issues are no longer important, and that love and romance are reserved for the young. Where these ideas come from is a mystery, and consist of a long list of the preconceived and incorrect notions that define ageism: the biased and inaccurate view that older adults are no longer relevant. It is a dismissive belief reflected in the attitudes we find in the workplace and the popular culture. Barusch (2009) says it well when she defines ageism as "a negative attitude toward older people and the process of aging, which manifests in subtle and varied ways. Ageism permeates our personal and cultural expectations of older adults. It is encountered whenever people of a certain age are considered too old to take a new job, to receive healthcare, or to fall in love" (p. 12).

This book is written to show how badly flawed and biased ageism is and to tell the growing numbers of older adults that they can enjoy love, intimacy, friendships and positive relationships with loved ones for many, many more years to come. Because I'm an older adult (69 when the book was written) and a current professor of social work, the book should not only give you a sense that I know something about aging but that I will approach the topics in the book in an objective way using the most current information available. I will also use stories from older adults. I hope you find the combination of objectivity and stories coupled with personal knowledge of aging a good fit. I promise I have written the book as I would want it written were I the reader—with an absence of jargon and psychobabble, problems that plague many books for older adults. Because I'm a social worker and we're very practical people, I'm going to offer suggestions that are based on common sense and the wisdom of the professionals who write about aging.

Here's a quote from one of those professionals who sums up my view of older adult intimacy: "Romantic love is a powerful force in human development, shaping the events of our lives and the people we become" (Barusch 2009, p. 12). The author continues by reporting the results of an Internet survey she conducted indicating that older adults "frequently experience intense infatuation at advanced ages. Results of our Internet survey suggest that adults over the age of 50 who were in new relationships experienced even greater romantic intensity than younger adults involved in new romances" (p. 12).

FAMILY AND FRIENDS

Older people have needs for other forms of intimacy. We want to be close to our loved ones, particularly our children and grandchildren, but too many of us suffer the pain of being marginalized by our children and left out of their lives. Rejection by our children is hurtful, perhaps even more hurtful than being rejected by the adult we love who no longer loves us because we helped create and raise our children. The adult child who never returns our phone calls, who never calls to find out how we are, who neglects to invite us to birthday parties and holiday meals, even when we live in the same community, is a hurt some of us never get over. What should we do? Hopefully this book will help you overcome hurt feelings and do something that will change the course of your relationships with your children, siblings, and extended family members.

It would be nice if blood really were thicker than water, but many of us have distant and unsatisfying relationships with our siblings. Why, we wonder, don't they call us on our birthdays when we always call them? Why don't they send a Christmas present when we always send one to them? Why do they invite other friends to join them on trips when we'd love to go but are never asked? I taught a class of 30 graduate social worker students a few years ago and asked if any of them were not on speaking terms with a brother or sister. Every single hand went up.

Half the older students said they hadn't spoken to a sibling in more than 10 years—some of them in more than 20 years. How could such a thing happen? I'll discuss why it happens and what we can do about it in a chapter on relationships with loved ones.

Friendships are important to everyone throughout the life span, but older adults who are single and living a distance from families rely on friends in very important ways. Whom do we go to when we have a crisis and we're not in a current love relationship? We often go to friends until we find out, as many of us have, that the people we think of as friends are just acquaintances who have only a marginal sense of loyalty to us. A friend once told me that he'd had a heart problem and called his best friend (he thought) to ask her to drive him to the ER. She said no, and as he drove himself to the ER with his heart rate beating at over 200 beats a minute, he wondered how he could have been so wrong about his supposed friend. It isn't until a crisis hits that we know who our friends really are. I will provide some objective information to those of you who have a hard time distinguishing real friends from acquaintances in a future chapter.

My immigrant mother was a fan of radio soap operas. She would listen to them and when an episode ended, she would come up with aphorisms that used to make me wince. One of her favorites was, "Better to have a good neighbor near by than family far away." Having worked her way across Europe for three years before she finally came to America, she knew something about loyalty and who you could trust. She had been in life-threatening situations and had learned that you have to develop a friendship slowly and over time, and that you should never take for granted that the other person felt about you the same way you felt about them. It seems like a good lesson for all the issues we'll talk about in this book.

STORIES

I asked a number of people to write stories for the book about love, romance, relationships with loved ones, and particularly relationships with children. I didn't ask them to be positive or negative but to write honestly about their experiences and to offer some advice that might help others. Each chapter has a story or two, all written by people in their sixties, seventies, and eighties. I haven't edited anything other than minor grammatical errors. Here's a story about conflict with a sibling many of you may find familiar.

PERSONAL STORY: SISTER CONFLICT

"I am the oldest of three children. My sister, Lorna, is four years younger than I am. We have a brother, Joe, who is the middle child—one year younger than me and three years older than my sister. My sister and I shared a bedroom while we grew up.

"The dynamics of our household were such that Lorna, the youngest child in our family, was our mother's favorite. I used to tell myself that even though I strongly sensed my mother's favoritism, I magnanimously did not take this perceived unfairness out on my sister. Not surprisingly, I suppose, she feels otherwise. I suppose it was inevitable that she and I had conflicts, especially since we shared a bedroom. It is unclear to me, looking back, how many of those conflicts were due simply to the usual sibling rivalry, our forced proximity in sharing a bedroom, or how much was due to what must have been my resentment of what I saw as her favored position in the family. Interestingly, my recollections are that things between us were usually hunky dory, while Lorna recollects terrible fights and my abuse of her.

"As to why Lorna was my mother's favorite, my mother told me a story several years before she died that may begin to explain some of her favoritism. She said that when she became pregnant with Lorna (who was named after her mother), our father announced he did not want a third child. A few days later he brought home some pills that he told my mother would induce a miscarriage, and told my mother to take them. My mother was horrified, and threw them out while pretending to take them. So I couldn't help but wonder if my mother felt a special affinity for Lorna because she felt she'd saved her life.

"I recall the following incident which, combined with previous incidents, made me feel like an outsider—an intruder—in my own home. Shortly after I had gone away to college, I returned home for the first time for Thanksgiving. When I walked into my bedroom, I discovered that Lorna had removed my bed and taken over all the drawers of my dresser. Not only had my sister drop-kicked me out of the house, my mother let her do it.

"Fast-forward to recent history. My sister is single and childless, having been married once very briefly. She has a career, a lakefront condo, and a large circle of friends. During most of my adulthood, even though my sister and I have lived some distance from each other, we have put these petty childhood conflicts behind us and been close but lately Lorna and I seem estranged for reasons I can't fully understand.

"I have been divorced twice and have one child and one grandchild. Around five years ago, I met a man with whom I am now living. I recently retired and we bought a house together and moved to Colorado.

"Lorna has a childhood friend, Marsha, who lives in Los Angeles, just a few miles from where I was living at the time. One Christmas Lorna announced she was coming out to L.A., but not to see me, but to see Marsha. While she was there we spent a few hours together, which felt obligatory, as if she were visiting me out of duty. I felt hurt. While she was in L.A. she presented me with a Christmas present that seemed odd—almost like it was something she had bought for herself and then didn't want. I was puzzled.

"The following year on my birthday she sent me a watch with a leather band that had obviously been previously worn. She regifted me. I was offended. There were a few other incidents involving either odd gifts, or no gifts. I then sent an email suggesting we refrain from sending birthday or Christmas gifts. I received no response at all to that email.

"Later she announced that she and Marsha were taking a trip together on a barge down the Danube River. She had received the trip as a bonus of sorts from her job, and she was entitled to bring a guest at no charge. I was hurt that she did not think to invite me.

"Recently, I sent Lorna an email expressing unhappiness and dismay at what I saw as the deterioration of our relationship. She responded by saying she was busy, and would respond to my email soon. I never received a response.

"This year I sent another email again suggesting we refrain from exchanging birthday presents (the birthdays of the three of us fall within a month of each other—what we call the 'birthday season'). This time she responded, wanting to know why I wished to do this. I hesitated responding, not quite sure what to say. I decided to be truthful about my feelings about her recent gifts, and again expressed my unhappiness about the state of our relationship. She sent a terse response, essentially saying, well fine, I guess that is your reality. This all occurred during our 'birthday season.' I wondered what would happen when my birthday rolled around in the next few weeks. I received no phone call, but the day after my birthday I received a card from Lorna closing with 'I love you.'

"I tend to obsess [over] a lot about things that hurt me and I've begun to wonder why Lorna and I are so estranged. Two things come to mind. When we were both single and before Michael came into my life, we talked about living together when we retired. I wonder if Lorna is angry about that or if she's jealous about the fact that I have someone in my life and she doesn't. Or maybe it's just the old conflicts we've always had, the ones from when we were kids, and maybe we'll never settle them. I don't know. All I know is that it hurts and there doesn't seem much that I can do about it except try to forget about it and get on with my life.

"Michael says that I should go get some professional help and maybe that would make it better. I'm thinking about it but until then I guess I'm just going to have to let Lorna do more of the work and, to the extent that I can, try not to let it bother me so much."—J. H. F.

SUMMARY

This chapter discusses the realities of love and intimacy with a number of important people in the lives of older adults, including people we are intimate with, family members and friends. The chapter notes that many of us have long-standing problems with family and friends and that mature love as we age sometimes eludes us. A personal story at the end of the chapter discusses the hurt associated with a younger sister who isn't responsive to the relationship desires of her older sister and why the older sister believes the conflict between them is happening now.

REFERENCES

Barusch, A. S. (2009). "Love and Ageism—A Social Work Perspective." *Social Work Today* 9 (1): 12.

Bean, J. F., Vora, A., and Frontera, W. R. (2004). "Benefits of Exercise for Community-dwelling Older Adults." *Archives of Physical Medicine and Rehabilitation* 85 (7 Suppl 3): S31–S42.

Cohen, G. D. (2005). *The Mature Mind: The Positive Power of the Aging Brain.* New York: Basic Books.

Emlet, C. A., and Poindexter, C. C. (2004). "Unserved, Unseen, and Unheard: Integrating Programs for HIV-infected and HIV-affected Older Adults." *Health and Social Work* 29 (2): 86–96.

Johnson, R. A. (1983). *We: Understanding the Psychology of Romantic Love.* New York: Harper Collins.

Levin, I. (2004). "Living Apart Together: A New Family Form." *Current Sociology* 52 (2): 223–40.

Pfeiffer, E., and Davis, G. C. (1974). "Determinants of Sexual Behavior in Middle and Old Age." In Palmore, E. (ed.), *Normal Aging II: Reports from the Duke Longitudinal Studies, 1970–1973.* Durham, NC: Duke University Press, 251–62.

Ray, R. (2008). *Endnotes: An Intimate Look at the End of Life.* New York: Columbia University Press.

Wechsler, D. (1955). *Manual for the Wechsler Adult Intelligence Scale.* New York: The Psychological Corporation.

CHAPTER 2

Mature Love

An unknown author wrote, "The question is asked 'Is there anything more beautiful in life than a young couple clasping hands and pure hearts in the path of marriage? Can there be anything more beautiful than young love?' "

And the answer is given: "Yes, there is a more beautiful thing. It is the spectacle of an old man and an old woman finishing their journey together on that path. Their hands are gnarled, but still clasped; their faces are seamed, but still radiant; their hearts are physically bowed and tired, but still strong with love and devotion for one another. Yes, there is a more beautiful thing than young love. Old love."

INTRODUCTION

Older adults experience love in a more accepting and emotionally healthy way than younger people. Older love is often more patient. Zernike (2007, p. 1) notes that for older adults, "As we experience the good and bad times, they're more precious, they're richer. It may also be true that older people are simply better able to deal with the emotional aspects of love. According to brain researchers, as the brain ages it becomes more programmed to be happy in relationships." Zernike adds,

As people get older, they seem to naturally look at the world through positivity and be willing to accept things that when we're young we would find disturbing and vexing. It is not rationalization: the reaction is instantaneous. Instead of what would be most disturbing for somebody, feeling betrayed or discomfort, the other thoughts—about how from his perspective it's not betrayal—can be accommodated much more easily, it paves the way for you to be sympathetic to the situation from his perspective, to be less disturbed from her perspective. (p. 1)

Walsh (1988) believes that married older couples often experience increased marital satisfaction and intimacy as they begin to realize that they have only a limited time left to be a couple. Of course there are also older adults who maintain troubled approaches to love, and "who are just as jealous, just as infantile, just as filled with irrationality when they fall in love in their 70s and 80s as [they were at earlier ages]. And it still is possible to have a broken heart in old age. A broken heart looks different in somebody old. You don't yell and scream like you might when you were 20" (Zernike 2007, p. 1).

Barusch (2009) interviewed a number of people ages 51–97. She found that those who were married or in committed relationships reported that love consistently improved with age. The author also found that people over 50 in new relationships reported higher romantic, physical, and emotional intensity than younger adults in new relationships. The author also found that the definition of love changed as people aged and included caretaking and less restricted gender roles. Men, in particular, craved additional intimacy as they aged. Intimacy issues, in the author's study, were broadly defined to include erotic love for some and chastity for others. Many of the people in her study were content with touching and hugs and other indicators of affection.

Khaleque (2003) found that intimate relationships with adults are one of the most important predictors of psychological adjustment in later life. Khaleque also suggests that past researchers have found that disruptions in early childhood attachments to parents may affect the quality of intimate relationships in later life. Rohner and Khaleque (2003) report that childhood experiences of parental acceptance-rejection have significant influence on partner acceptance-rejection and, even in later life, we often choose intimate partners based on the patterns of acceptance-rejection by parents we experienced in childhood. Because we often outgrow these early patterns in those we seek to have intimacy with, it may help explain why older love differs from younger love in that we seek people who are more truly our *bishert*, our chosen ones.

OLDER LOVE AND INTIMACY

Many older adults experience a remarkable renewal of intimacy and come to value a mature notion of love that is more accepting and emotionally healthy than ideas of love they might have had when they were younger. Older love is often more patient. Older adults recognize that the bad times pass and the good times pass. "As you experience the good and bad times, they're more precious, they're richer" (Zernike 2007, p. 1). It's also true that older people may simply be better able to deal with the emotional aspects of love. As it ages, the brain becomes more programmed to be happy in relationships, according to brain researchers.

Regarding older adult intimacy, Stein (2007) reports the results of a study of 3,000 U.S. adults ages 57–85. The study found that half to three-quarters of the respondents remained sexually active, with a "significant population engaging in frequent and varied sex" (p. A1). The study found that physically healthier people reported the highest rates of sexual activity and that a healthy sex life may itself help keep people vibrant. According to Stein, the study noted that 28 percent of the men and 14 percent of the women said sex was very important and those with partners reported being sexually active as often as people in their forties and early fifties, "but even among the oldest age group (80–85), 54 percent of those who were sexually active reported having sex at least two to three times per month and 23 percent reported having sex once a week or more" (p. A1).

INFATUATION

Most of us think of infatuation as a prelude to love, but a number of authors and researchers view infatuation as a negative emotional experience. For example, Drew (2009) defines infatuation as "a static process characterized by an unrealistic expectation of blissful passion without positive growth and development. Characterized by a lack of trust, lack of loyalty, lack of commitment, lack of reciprocity, an infatuation is not necessarily foreplay for a love scenario" (p. 1). Peach (2009) writes that infatuation is often called being "a fool in love" and is usually seen as "a state in which a person's normal ability to think clearly and act rationally are flung aside with suspicious eagerness. Desire focuses on a particular someone and suddenly nothing matters but that compelling attraction" (p. 1).

In discussing the difference between love and infatuation Drew suggests that with infatuation the faults you refused to see when the relationship was new will became obvious but with love, "our focus is on your special someone, and that someone exists in the real world. Give and take, compromise and cooperation are characteristics of love relationships. Working toward common goals, sharing dreams and values define the dynamics of a good love relationship. People know each other on a separate and private level than the world at large" (p. 2).

Barusch (2009) believes that American culture puts a great deal of weight on infatuation, often giving it a major role in the way we think about romance. We often believe that infatuation is the initial experience we feel that will result in a long-term commitment. Although most older adults know that infatuation is a temporary state, it's easy to forget that when you're in its grip. Barusch writes about a client in his late fifties who planned to leave his wife of 30 years for a new love:

> Over a period of several months, he spoke for hours at a time about this infatuation. Later, he told me I had saved his marriage with one statement. As he fantasized about life with his beloved, I asked about his children, wondering whether his new love would be as interested in his children as their mother and how that might play out when grandchildren came along. He felt this conversation was a tipping point, setting the stage for the infatuation's slow fade. Eventually, he was able to rededicate himself to the marriage. (p. 12)

THE PHASES OF INFATUATION

Peach (2009) believes that infatuation has the following phases:

INFATUATION PHASE I: STRICKEN!

This takes place when we suddenly realize that someone has special meaning to us. Many of us find this a special moment.

INFATUATION PHASE II: INTRUSIVE THINKING

In the second phase of infatuation we can't stop thinking about that person and looking forward to our next meeting.

Infatuation Phase III: Idealization

The third phase takes place when we so idealize the person with whom we're infatuated with that we can't see any flaws or potential problems and begin to view them with complete abandon as being perfect for us.

Infatuation Phase IV: The Emotional Rollercoaster

In Phase IV we vacillate between highs and lows with unrealistic expectations followed by doubts and nagging fears. Often we obsess about whether the other person is being faithful to us and whether we're foolish to feel so strongly when perhaps the other person doesn't share similar feelings. For many of us it is a time when we feel that love is poetic and, as often, frantic. I've worked with hardened prisoners who write poetry to the ones they love during this stage of infatuation. Almost all of us are susceptible to infatuation because it so heightens our senses.

ON MATURE LOVE

The following is my (the author's) belief about mature love.

When I think of mature love I think of two people who feel comfortable with one another. They can talk, plan, touch, be intimate, and carry positive feelings for each other through disagreements and times of stress. They protect one another from the fear of being alone and without anyone to support them in a health crisis. They know each other's emotional blind spots and accept their partners for who they are, not who they wish they were. They are grounded in the present. Instead of bringing up old experiences that involve other people in the past, they focus on the here and now rather than the then and there. They don't make unrealistic demands on each other but use gentle persuasion to help their partners see blind spots that may sometimes interfere in the relationship.

When times are tough in the relationship, as they sometimes are, people in a mature relationship play fair. They don't use tactics that hurt the relationship irreparably just for the sake of winning. They think of themselves as "us" rather than "me and you." They appreciate the talents and abilities of their partners and encourage and support growth. In a mature relationship there are no stars but instead two partners who work and play together rather than two separate people living their own lives.

Mature love means equality. It means that while one person may do better in certain areas of the relationship or have special skills, when everything is tallied, up the contribution of each partner to the relationship is equal. Mature love means that time is spent understanding the special abilities of each partner so that those abilities serve to strengthen the relationship. Mature love means never using sarcasm or embarrassing a partner in public. And unlike the book and film *Love Story*, which said that loving means never having to say you're sorry, mature love means saying you're sorry every five minutes, if necessary. In a mature relationship, apologizing should come easily, and it should always come from the heart.

If your partner has had children by someone other than you, mature love means treating those children as if they were your own—with love, tenderness, and concern. It means never criticizing your partner's children because it's hurtful and there are better ways to share your feelings. Mature love means understanding that you and your partner each have the need to be alone with your own children and that giving your partner the time and space to be together, even if it means a week or more without your partner, is part of the responsibility of being older adults in a loving and tender relationship.

Mature love means that you are both involved in keeping the relationship vital and interesting. This doesn't mean that you have to hop around the world or be on the go all the time. It means that relationships become stale in time if two people aren't equally involved in activities that are fun, challenging, and memorable. The mate who always plans while his or her partner goes along is not taking responsibility to keep the relationship alive, Similarly, passive people add nothing to relationships.

Mature love means that you plan to be with your partner through sickness and ill health—no fudging on this one. Mature love means that you have anticipated the many things that can happen to older people and you have made a commitment to your partner and to yourself—a sacred vow, really—that no matter what, you'll be there for them. Otherwise, you're just playing at love and you have an exit strategy. That isn't mature love; it's adolescent love. It's the type of love that results in breakups, divorces, hurt feelings, and broken hearts. It has no place in the world of mature love. Unless you make a pledge to your loved one that you will be there for them, no matter what, you can't call your relationship mature *or* loving. If you have an exit strategy you should call the relationship exactly what it is: temporary, uncommitted, and separate.

Mature love is based in reality. Most of us, after a certain age, don't walk along the beach hand in hand watching the sunset and then have drinks over a candlelit dinner before making love while listening to the waves washing against the beach. Sometimes we do, of course, but you can't do that every night or think of love as something out of a bad romance novel. Mature love is based on deep feelings of affection and warmth, not walks along the beach. I think most of us know this, but unfortunately too many older people base their notions of love and romance on the popular culture rather than the wisdom of older men and women whose relationships have lasted and prospered.

Most of all, mature love means that you can become old together and not worry about your loved one becoming emotionally and physically detached because they no longer find you interesting or attractive. Mature people recognize that aging is an equal opportunity employer; as you age and you want your loved one to continue finding you attractive, your partner has the same need. Flirting, carrying on relationships behind your mate's back, or having secret friendships are hurtful and are just not part of a mature relationship. There are rules of civility that apply in mature love. If you can't accept the rules and you still think of yourself as an older adolescent, you will not be able to call a relationship mature or loving.

In summary, as my daughter Amy wrote, "Many of us are overwhelmed with our daily workloads and feel unable to make long-term, far-reaching changes in our close relationships. But I believe that each of us has a gift that we can use to make our relationships better than they are. The task is simply to discern what our gifts are and to utilize them. Because, in the end, we are each our own Tooth Fairies, taking what has been lost and giving gold in return" (Glicken 2005, p. 310).

MATURE LOVE: RESOLVING A SERIOUS PROBLEM IN A RELATIONSHIP

The following e-mails were written over the course of three days as two older adults tried to work through a serious breach in their relationship caused by continual arguments over the prior month.

The first e-mail was sent to Lou from Phyllis after a continuation of a prior argument:

E-Mail 1: From Phyllis (Saturday Morning)

Lou,

The incidents of the past few weeks have made it painfully clear to me that we need to separate. I am communicating here with you via email, against your instructions, because I am at this point simply unable to fight with you any longer. I just can't do it and I can't live like this any longer. I just don't feel that you would talk to me the way you do if you respected me. I need to feel respected.

One of us needs to move out, and I think it should be you for a number of reasons.

1. You know nothing about, and have little interest in, maintaining this house.
2. You have someplace to go, namely Jennifer's [his daughter's] house. She has a guest room and a guest bath. If I were to leave, I would have nowhere to go. Barbara's [her daughter's] house is nine hours away, and they have no guest room.
3. You could take your laptop with you and continue to do whatever work you need to do. I have no laptop.

If you refuse to leave, I will do so.

I am leaving for the day today, and my strong suggestion is that when I return you will be gone. If you are not, I will pack my things and leave.

I want some peace.

I do love you.

E-Mail 2: From Lou (Saturday Evening)

I'm at Jennifer's [his daughter's] house now. I'm really tired and sad. I'll write more tomorrow. Lou

E-Mail 3: From Phyllis (Monday Morning)

You didn't write me yesterday.

E-Mail 4: From Lou (Monday Afternoon)

Yes, but when Sunday came around I didn't quite know what to say. You said you wanted some peace and I guess I felt that I should respect that and, if and when you wanted to talk, that I'd be available. I'm going out for coffee now but I'll be home at about three. Lou

E-Mail 5: From Phyllis (Monday Afternoon)

I don't know what to say either. It just seems futile to keep saying the same things I've said before, over and over, and nothing really changes. I don't know what to do. I miss you terribly, but I just can't have these things keep happening over, and over, and over. Something has to change. There were three "incidents" in a span of about two weeks. It seemed like we spent most of those two weeks in stony silence with each other, me with my stomach churning. It is unbearable. P

E-Mail 6: From Lou (Monday Afternoon)

I wrote you a long e-mail but it doesn't seem to have gone out. What I said was that I think I should come home, maybe Wednesday if that's OK. I miss you and I feel deeply saddened by what's happening to us. When I think about our fights it always seems after the fact to be about something pretty insignificant. It's hard to resolve things long distance and my best thought is that maybe you can call Karen [a couples counselor the two had been seeing] and set up an appointment. I'm not sure she's there this week but it's worth trying and in the meantime, I truly think we have to talk and strengthen our commitment and work to resolve whatever it is that's going wrong. I care about you deeply and it saddens me that we keep having such difficulties. I want to resolve them, for certain. Love, Lou

E-Mail 7: From Phyllis (Monday Evening)

Our fights are always about something trivial. Always. What the fight is about isn't the point, as I'm sure you know. It's your short fuse, and your tendency to talk down to me, or scold. But if that's all it was, it'd be nothing. It's the temper, and what I see as your extreme overreaction to trivial disagreements. And three episodes of anger and prolonged silences in a short period of time just sort of broke me. Perhaps these things bother me much more than they bother you.

I too care for you deeply, and if I lost you I don't know what I'd do. But I just don't know what to do about this.

I called Karen and left a message.

Of course you can come home Wednesday. I miss you terribly.

Love, Phyllis

E-Mail 8: From Lou (Monday Evening)

I'm certainly willing to listen openly to anything you have to say about me or any observations you have (I don't disagree with anything you said about my behavior). I think we need to go back to our five p.m. chats and use them to clear the air. I've been playing tennis with Owen [his son-in-law] in the mornings so I will likely be home Wednesday before five. I love you. I'll see you Wednesday afternoon.

I love you, Lou

POST SCRIPT

When Lou got home he and Phyllis had a very long talk. They agreed to develop some rules about miscommunications and to work very hard with the couples counselor to resolve their problems. They realized during the time they were apart that they loved one another deeply and that they wanted the relationship to succeed. With some hard work, counseling, and couples work, six months after this exchange of e-mails they're both doing very well.

SUMMARY

This chapter discusses mature love and the differences between infatuation, love with an exit strategy, and mature love. Mature love is love that grows slowly and builds into a positive, long-term, honest and loyal adult love. Infatuation is the high many of us experience when we first meet someone who totally involves us but begins to wither as we get to know that person better and see the flaws that make mature love unlikely. Love with an exit strategy is love with limits. The chapter ends with an exchange of e-mails during a troubled time in an older adult relationship.

REFERENCES

Bancroft, J. H. J. (2007). "Sex and Aging." http://cas.umkc.edu/casww/sa/Sex.htm.

Drew, M. "Love vs. Infatuation." Retrieved June 23, 2009 from: http://www.mental-health-matters.com/articles/article.php?artID=853.

Erikson, E. H. (1963). *Childhood and Society* (2nd ed.). New York: Norton.

Genevay, B. (1999). "Intimacy and Older People: Much More than Sex." *Dimensions* 6 (3).

Huffstetler H. (Spring 2006). "Sexuality in Older Adults: A Deconstructionist Perspective." *ADULTSPAN* 5 (1): 4–14.

Kaas, M. J. (1981). "Geriatric Sexuality Breakdown Syndrome." *International Journal of Aging and Human Development* 13: 71–77.

Khalegue, A. (2003). "Intimate Adult Relationships, Quality of Life and Psychological Adjustment." *Social Indicators Research* 69: 351–60.

The National Council on the Aging. (September 1998). *Healthy Sexuality and Vital Aging. Executive Summary*, 1–3.

Peach, D. "Infatuation." Retrieved February 6, 2009 from: http://www.sosuave.com/articles/infatuation.htm.

Perman, D. (February 2, 2006). "The Changing Face of Romance in 2006: Are Valentines Just for the Young?" *Intimacy and Aging: Tips for Sexual Health and Happiness. UBC Reports* 52 (2).

Rohner, R. P., and Khaleque, A. (2003). "Relations between Partner Acceptance and Parental Acceptance, Behavioral Control, and Psychosocial Adjustment among Heterosexual Adult Women." Unpublished manuscript.

Stein, R. (August 23, 2007). "Elderly Staying Sexually Active." *Washington Post.* http://www.washingtonpost.com/wp-dyn/content/article/2007/08/22/AR2007082202000_pf.html.

Walsh, F. (1988). "The Family in Later Life." In B. Carter and M. McGoldrick (eds.), *The Changing Family Life Cycle* (2nd ed.), 311–32. New York: Gardner.

Zernike, K. (November 18, 2007). "Still Many-Splendored: Love in the Time of Dementia." *New York Times.* http://query.nytimes.com/gst/fullpage.html?res=9D01E2D91030F93BA25752C1A9619C8B63&sec=&spon=&pagewanted=all.

CHAPTER 3

Understanding Men and Their Relationship Problems

INTRODUCTION

So many older women complain that their husbands, brothers, male friends, and boyfriends have trouble relating that I thought it might be helpful to include a chapter giving some of the reasons. It's important to note that as men age they often develop much better relationship skills, but many men don't. This is not to bash men but to help male and female readers understand.

As an example of the way men relate, I recently went to a Paella dinner with Flamenco music and dancing at my local tennis club. The food was great and the Flamenco dancing and music were excellent. As I looked around the room at the men and women I was struck by how excited, talkative, and appreciative the women were and how bored, quiet, and negative most of the men were. Since these were all men in their sixties and seventies, it made an impression. I tried to carry on a conversation with the husband of a lady sitting next to me. She was chatty, friendly, gregarious, and fun while her husband was emotionless and didn't say a word throughout dinner. The fellow sitting a few chairs from me didn't change his expression of mild contempt throughout the evening. Most of the men looked bored and almost none of them said a word. How could that be when the evening was so much fun? Hopefully, you'll find a few reasons in the following discussion.

THE MALE CODE OF CONDUCT:
WHAT EVERY MAN KNOWS

Some of the following material comes from the author's book on men (Glicken 2005).

No one sits down with the men of America and teaches them a male code of conduct, yet most men know the code fairly early in life and try to live by it. They know, for example, that men who give in to pain are considered to be unmanly by other men, and that after a certain age you're not supposed to cry, ever. Men know that an unwillingness to compete is often seen as a sign of weakness by other men, even for older men who may be suffering from medical problems that make it unwise for them to compete in sports or other activities and ventures. Whatever the situation might be, there is an unspoken expectation that men will often try to outdo one another. Not to be competitive and not to try to win are considered signs of weakness. Above all, the positive judgments of other men are profoundly important.

Many of the messages men learn are first given in sports, where men are taught about winning and superiority. Sports have always been an acceptable way for men to show their dominance over others. Scher (1979) writes that "Men learn early in life to compete with their fellows. Their need to win is pervasive" (p. 253). Brannon (1976) believes that there are four primary messages given to men at such an early age that, even before puberty, boys know the messages well enough to have mastered them to some extent. The primary male messages are:

1. No Sissy Stuff: the need to be different from women.
2. The Big Wheel: the need to be superior to others.
3. The Sturdy Oak: the need to be self-reliant and independent.
4. Give 'em Hell: the need to be more powerful than others, through violence if necessary.

When boys are unable to master these primary male messages, they learn to compensate through exaggerated male behavior, or what Tiller (1967) calls "compensatory masculinity." The boy striving to become a man who also feels fearful and insecure in the process may copy male verbal patterns or the way men he admires walk. Boys see the imitation of men they admire as a way of proving to others that *they* are men. Boys may drink or smoke at an early age to exaggerate their need to be seen as manly. When the need to prove their masculinity is overpowering, compensatory masculinity may lead young boys into violence or extreme risk-taking. It is no small coincidence that violence and risk-taking among very young boys are often found in chaotic families or families where fathers have abandoned their children.

Bereska (2003) believes that male messages are remarkably unchanged since the Victorian period. She notes that the boy's world is still "characterized by certain types and degrees of emotional expression, naturalized aggression, male hang-out groups, hierarchies within those groups, competition, athleticism, sound moral character, and adventure. It is heterosexual, comprised of active male bodies, and no sissies are allowed" (p. 168). Yacovene (1990) agrees and writes, "The social roles of men and women have changed dramatically since the early nineteenth century, yet the cultural perceptions of masculinity have remained remarkable static" (p. 85).

THE FOUR THEMES OF MALE DEVELOPMENT

Let's consider Brannon's four primary messages learned in childhood, when and how they are given, and their impact on male behavior.

NO SISSY STUFF: THE NEED TO BE DIFFERENT FROM WOMEN

Boys are taught to be different from girls almost immediately. Parents who try to encourage boys to be sensitive and to recognize their feminine side often fight an uphill battle. Boys teach one another the messages and beliefs they learn from older boys, while the media transmits male role expectations. Men subtly influence boys to be stoic and not to give into to pain. No pain, no gain; it is a message that is given to men by every athletic coach who has ever lived and one reinforced by every man who plays team sports and by every fan who watches. Men play hurt. Men make pain a mark of manliness. Where men are taught to control and deny feelings, women are often taught to express them.

As boys mature into young men, this message becomes a code of conduct. "If you can't take the heat, get out of the kitchen." The messages we pass on to young men are messages of strength and endurance, of mastery of pain, of bravery and selflessness; these are male codes of conduct that American men are so well steeped in that most boys have mastered them by the time they reach adolescence, if not earlier.

A significant message that men are given is that they are different from women in very fundamental ways. Where women are weak physically and emotionally, men are tough. Where women cry, men never do. Where women give up easily, men never give up. These messages of strength versus weakness are given to boys early in life, and boys experiencing failure in school often believe that the educational superiority of girls is another example of gender differences and often come to believe that education is a feminine attribute. This may explain the failure of men to seek college educations, develop intellectual curiosity, and the general superiority of women academically.

Many of the male codes of conduct may be explained by genetic differences and predispositions of men. For example, male infants suffer higher rates of illness and behavioral problems than female infants.

THE BIG WHEEL: THE NEED TO BE SUPERIOR TO OTHERS AT ANY COST

"Winning isn't something," said one of America's great coaches, "it's everything." "It isn't about winning or losing," said another American sage, "it's always about winning." And so it is, because boys are told in small and large ways that being first, winning, and being better than anyone else is what men strive for in sports, at work, and in love—even older men. When women ask men why they have so few friends, it's difficult to have friends when you're always trying to outdo the other person. Writing about the need men have to be superior to others, Cowley (2003) says, "The drive for dominance skews our perceptions, colors our friendships, shapes our moods, and affects our [men's] health" (p. 67). The put-downs and sarcasm that sometimes characterize male behavior with other men is not meant to bring men closer together but is, instead, meant to prove to others that a man is stronger, smarter, tougher, and more attractive to women, by far, than any other man alive. But I should add that the need to be superior also serves to draw other men closer to one another. By showing that a man is better than anyone else, it also suggests that he is a leader.

THE STURDY OAK: THE NEED TO BE SELF-RELIANT AND INDEPENDENT

When you observe very young boys at play, you will notice that their play is sometimes solitary. It will tell you how well the culture trains its boys for independence. Expecting men to be cooperative and good team players is often not a part of the social and cultural training that explains male behavior. In earlier times in our history, self-reliance and independence were necessary for survival and were considered positive male attributes. Only recently have men have been criticized for being bad team players and too uncooperative for modern corporate or bureaucratic life. Modern life demands cooperation, while men have been taught to be solitary players. Men often resent supervision. "Give me a job," they will tell you, "and let me do it." Consider this conversation among some construction workers, overheard at the author's favorite morning coffee spot.

> The foreman I had on the last job, he let us alone. Do your work, he said, be on time, get it done right. You know how to do it, so do it. We got the project done in no time. Got bonus points for getting it done early. It was great. We all felt like he respected us. But this guy now, he can't let anything happen without poking his big nose into it. Leave us alone. We know our job, I tell him, but he just keeps on bugging us. One of the guys punched him out last week. They were gonna can him but the union saved him. It's been a lot better on the job now. You gotta respect a man and leave him alone. Everybody knows that.

While this may be an extreme example, we know that men need to develop cooperative skills if they are to be successful in the workplace and in relationships. One way of accomplishing cooperation is what Svoboda (2002) calls independence with boundaries or "sponsored independence." Independence with boundaries provides an opportunity for men to develop independently without losing closeness to others while at the same time gaining skills in cooperative endeavors. Men are given room to develop their own personalized ways of doing things while being encouraged to share those ways with others by accepting that the process may lead to acceptance or rejection of their ideas, but never of them personally.

GIVE 'EM HELL: THE NEED TO BE MORE POWERFUL THAN OTHERS, THROUGH VIOLENCE IF NECESSARY

Boys are often taught that if someone challenges them, they must fight back. If they don't fight back it may be interpreted as a sign of weakness. Fights abound in the lives of young boys. This behavior continues through young adulthood and sometimes beyond. It is no doubt one of the reasons for high rates of juvenile violence and the spread of gang violence in many American cities. The stories men tell are all about giving the people around them hell. The author was told the following story by a colleague in his early sixties, proving that education, rank, and age do not eliminate the need for men to give people who cross them a piece of their minds (and their bodies) if necessary.

> I was doing some consulting for a small college in the Midwest. I'd go out there every few months and the dean I was to work with would torpedo everything I did. I'd order something done and then when I left, he'd countermand it. All he had was criticism for my work, but it was the kind that was petty and unimportant. Little academic put-downs. Finally, we had a confrontation, really nasty. He actually threatened to fight me. I couldn't believe it. This little middle-aged guy, very academic, he actually wanted to duke it out with me. I stood up when he challenged me. I'm at least a foot taller and 50 pounds heavier, but this guy stood up and made a fist like he's going to hit me. Finally, I started to laugh and walked away. They removed him, of course, but it seemed so like our society. Even older educated men, when everything else fails, can resort to violence. It made me wonder how far we've really come.

UNDERSTANDING MALE DEVELOPMENT

Male Training to Be Men

O'Neil (1981) believes that men are taught a number of propositions that form their understanding of the "masculine mystique," including the notions that

> power, dominance, competition, and control are necessary to proving one's masculinity; that vulnerabilities, feelings, and emotions in men are signs of femininity and are to be avoided; that masculine control of self, others, and environment are essential for men to feel safe, secure, and comfortable; and that men seeking help and support from others show signs of weakness, vulnerability, and potential incompetence. (Robertson and Fitzgerald 1992, p. 241)

One result of the need to be independent is that men often have few support systems and a very limited number of friends. In his book

Man Enough, Pitman is quoted by the editors of *Voice Male* magazine as writing, "sometimes there is something that a man needs to reveal, needs to talk over with another man, and there may be no man available to him. Sometimes, manhood is lonely. . . . Loneliness is what it costs a man to be true to his code of masculinity. Many such men, under the sway of the masculine mystique, lead shockingly lonely lives" (*Voice Male* 2001, p. 10).

Scher (1979) believes that changes in society have placed men in uncomfortable roles. While men are expected to always be strong, healthy, sexually robust, and tireless, the impossibility of this creates a great deal of posing, deception, and failure. As society continues to expect men to be strong, it criticizes them for all of the attributes it expects of them, producing a confusing set of expectations that often lead to physical and emotional difficulty. Scher says that this ambiguity is difficult for most men to cope with and writes, "Many of the attitudes that provided stability are now disintegrating and men are clinging to them in an attempt to maintain order. But their clinging only creates more problems" (Scher 1979, p. 252).

Notman (1991) believes that from the very beginning of life, parents relate in the following very different ways to male and female children: "They speak differently, have different expectations, and present them with different communications and sets of signals and directions, which infants and children absorb and use as they build up mental representations of themselves" (p. 120). Kohlberg (1987) found that a young boy's fear of being a sissy is more intense than a girl's fear of being a tomboy. Social pressure from parents, teachers, and peers provide different environments for boys and girls. Kohlberg believed that boys are socialized differently, given different messages than girls, and have internalized those values and messages into their own value system. As examples of male socialization, Kohlberg notes that boys are encouraged to play rough, to not cry, and to be strong and courageous.

As boys enter adolescence and then young adulthood, peers become a strongly influential force in defining a man's identity. For most white males, finding a work identity seems to be much easier than establishing intimate relationships (Rabinowitz and Cochran 1994). Because many young men have a limited understanding of more intimate relationships with women, a type of "feminine mystique" sometimes develops that characterizes women as having certain mysterious powers (Pleck 1987). Pleck describes two types of power men perceive women to have over them. The first is expressive power, or the power to express emotions. Since women are given permission to express emotions, a man may depend on a woman to express his emotions for him. If the woman refuses to exercise her expressive role, the man will try harder to get the woman to play this role. The second power Pleck describes is masculinity-validating power. In order for a male to experience himself as being masculine, the female is encouraged to play her scripted role in doing those things that make him feel masculine. Once again, when a woman refuses to engage in this role, the man may try to force the woman back into her traditional role, sometimes through the use of coercion, manipulation, or violence.

Rigid notions of male roles tend to modify themselves in middle age when men begin to integrate both male and female definitions of their roles (Levinson et al. 1978). The authors believe that with age, men shift from traditional male roles to being more nurturing and concerned about the quality of relationships. O'Neil and Egan (1992) report that age modifies traditional views of male gender roles and that men begin to experience less role conflict in some areas of life as they mature. But Mahalik and colleagues (2001) believe that if traditional male role models do not modify themselves as men age that they will negatively affect feelings of intimacy and self-esteem.

GENETIC FACTORS IN MALE DEVELOPMENT

Genetic factors may also explain differences between male and female behavior. Parker and colleagues (1999) report very different levels of ability in male and female children to use emotional language from an early age. The inability to communicate emotions causes young boys to feel uncomfortable and ill at ease, but not to really know why—a condition many counselors find in adult male clients. Fivush (1989) found that boys show signs of significant anger by age three, a finding not found with three-year-old girls. A related finding is that when boys are exposed to the distress of others, they seem far less concerned than girls. Fabes and colleagues (1994) report that in a group of six-year-old boys and girls listening to a recording of a crying baby, more girls showed concern for the baby's distress, while twice as many boys just turned the speakers off. Physical examinations showed the boys to be more anxious over the child's crying and more intolerant of the crying than girls.

Other signs of genetic differences are reported by Keller and West (1995), who found that boys and girls react differently to early separation and bereavement. Boys showed little concern while girls were often highly preoccupied with them. The authors indicate that while neither response is necessarily healthy, the response by the young boys is in keeping with the tendency for males not to know how they feel emotionally and not to ask for help when it may be needed. This early behavior in boys to deny feelings and to avoid asking for help very likely carries on into adulthood. Rout (1999) reports that male British physicians (general practitioners in this study) were more anxious and depressed than female doctors, but were also more likely to avoid contact with other people when stressed, and not to seek help.

A number of researchers make strong arguments that male physiology is the primary reason for many of the differences between men and women. An example of the way physical differences affect adults is provided by Kraemer (2000), who believes that early behaviors of young boys have a consistent physiological pattern that continues to affect men throughout their lives. The author writes,

> Even when ill, men may not notice signs of illness, and when they do they are less likely to seek help from doctors. This tendency will account for some of the excess suicides in males. In his despair the victim believes that no help is available, that talking is useless. If baby boys are typically harder to care for it is arguable that they will be more likely to feel lonely as adults. (Kraemer 2000, 1611)

Kraemer also reports that male infants tend to be much more excitable than female infants and that mothers spend considerable time soothing the male infant's anxiety at some expense to normal development. Murray (1998) found that young boys were very affected by the moods of their mothers. In mothers suffering from postpartum depression, the impact lasted well into kindergarten and long after the mother's depression had lifted.

Kraemer (2000) believes that serious accidents among boys are largely related to poor motor skills and cognitive abilities that place boys at higher risk for accidents than girls. When compensatory masculinity and lower socioeconomic status are added to genetic predispositions, the result is a dramatic increase in violence, suicide, drug and alcohol usage and other unhealthy behaviors.

Hopkins and Bard (1993) have shown that girls have better literary skills than boys and are more adept at using language. This may explain why girls continue to surpass boys academically. The authors also report that "alexithymia"—the lack of an emotional vocabulary—is much more common in boys and may help to explain the difficulty men have in expressing intimate feelings. The authors believe that these differences are seen very early in life and that one cannot argue that socialization alone is responsible. As Kraemer (2000) indicates:

> Even from conception, before social effects come into play, males are more vulnerable than females. Social attitudes about the resilience of boys compound the biological deficit. Male mortality is greater than female mortality throughout life. The causes are a mixture of biological and social pressures: we need to be aware of both in order to promote better development and health for boys and men. (p. 1611)

Male infants often require considerably more attention than female infants and are more distressed when attention isn't given. Sackett (1972) has studied this same phenomenon in male rhesus monkeys, partially or totally isolated from maternal care, and found that they are far more likely to "freeze" in test situations than are matched females, who are more active and curious.

Wilson (1993) points out that in the argument over temperament versus socialization, even in Japanese preschools where sympathy and concern for others followed by cooperation are emphasized, the same gender differences are seen in both Japanese and American preschools: "The boys acted like warriors, the girls like healers and peacemakers" (p. 27).

CONFLICT BETWEEN MEN AND WOMEN

Brooks (1990) points out that an additional issue in male development affecting the way men interact with women is gender role strain, or what Brooks defines as "the discomfort resulting from disharmony between early gender socialization and newer role expectations" (p. 52). When gender role strain is minimal, as it is with men trying to understand their relationships with loved ones and friends and doing so in a sensitive and thoughtful way, the strain results in better male-female relationships. In more "traditional" men, "role strain may be more intense, destructive, and devoid of benefits than the strain experienced by other men" (Brooks 1990, p. 52). Brooks defines traditional men as competitive, stoic, homophobic, aloof in their fathering roles, neglectful of their health needs, and distrusting women while at the same time over-relying on them on them for "nurturance, emotional expressiveness, and validation of masculinity" (p. 51). Pleck (1980) believes that men need the approval of women to feel masculine and that they are highly dependent on women for feelings of self-worth and achievement.

Pleck (1987) also believes that "men as a group are experiencing more psychological distress than they did three decades ago, both absolutely and relative to women" (p. 20). According to Pleck, many aspects of traditional male-female relationships are unacceptable to women and create conflict in traditional men who see no personal benefit in having more equal relationships with women. Traditional men rarely see any point in changing what they expect in a relationship. When change is demanded, as in the case of abusive behavior or the possibility of divorce, Scher (1990) says that traditional men see few "life-enhancing qualities in psychotherapy and come into therapy because they have no alternative" (p. 3).

Another area of gender role strain is what Spielberg (1993) describes as the need for men to define themselves in heroic ways. By "heroic," Spielberg means that men have traditionally seen themselves as "righteous warriors" whose behavior is defined by acts of bravery and good deeds. As men experience more confusion over the meaning of the word "heroic," Spielberg believes that men have not been able to adequately respond "to the dilemma of a loss of a guiding image of manhood" (p. 173).

COMMON HEALTH PROBLEMS OF MEN

One of the significant ways the health of men impacts relationships is that men have much higher rates of health problems than women, largely because they don't take care of themselves and seldom see doctors until their health is in jeopardy. This makes loved ones instant caretakers. The following discussion provides a brief description of how poor men's health has become.

In reporting data from the University of Michigan's Institute for Social Research, Gupta (2003) notes that, "men outrank women in all of the 15 leading causes of death, except one: Alzheimer's. Men's death rates are at least twice as high as women's for suicide, homicide and cirrhosis of the liver" (p. 84). The principle researcher on the study of men's health, David Williams, says that men are twice as likely to be heavy drinkers and to "engage in behaviors that put their health at risk, from abusing drugs to driving without a seat belt"

(Gupta 2003, p. 84). Gupta goes on to note that men are more often involved in risky driving and that SUV rollovers and motorcycle accidents largely involve men. Williams blames this behavior on, "deep-seated cultural beliefs—a 'macho' world view that rewards men for taking risks and tackling danger head on" (Gupta 2003, p. 84).

Further examples of risky male behavior leading to injury and death include the fact that men are twice as likely to get hit by lightning or die in a flash flood, and are more likely to drive around barricades resulting in more deaths by train accidents and drowning in high water. As a significant difference in the way men and women approach their health, Gupta indicates that women are twice as likely as men to visit their doctors once a year and are more likely to explore broad-based preventive health plans with their physician than men. Men are less likely to schedule checkups or to follow up when symptoms arise. Men also tend to internalize their emotions and self-medicate their psychological problems, notes Williams, while women tend to seek professional help. Virtually all stress-related diseases—from hypertension to heart disease—are more common in men.

American men between the ages of 45 and 64 suffer an estimated 218,000 heart attacks a year, compared with 74,000 a year for women in the same age group, one of many reasons women live more than 7 years longer than men (*Drug Store News* 1998). Epperly and Moore (2000) report that men are at much greater risk of alcohol abuse than women, with the highest rates of alcoholism occurring in men between 25 and 39 years of age. However, age is not a deterrent for risk factors in men, and 14 percent of men over 65 are alcohol-dependent, as compared to 1.5 percent of women in the same age group. Suicides in men over 65 are six times the rate of the general population, according to Reuben and colleagues (1996).

These findings of greater health problems among men are not explained by biological differences related to gender. Harrison, Chin, and Ficarrotto (1988) write that "Research suggests that it is not so much biological gender that is potentially hazardous to men's health but rather specific behaviors that are traditionally associated with male sex roles which can be (but in the case of women are not) taken on by either gender."

Saunders (2000) reports that a poll by Louis Harris and associates in May and November 1998 indicated that 28 percent of the men as compared to 8 percent of the women had not visited a physician in the prior year. While 19 percent of the women didn't have a regular physician, 33 percent of men didn't have one either. More than half of the men surveyed had not been tested for cholesterol or had a physical examination in the prior year. Waiting as long as possible to receive needed medical care was a strategy used by a fourth of the men studied, and only 18 percent of the men surveyed sought medical care immediately when a medical problem arose.

Additional health data paint an equally troubling picture of male health. *Drug Store News* (1998) reported the following information for American pharmacists: (1) Women still outlive men by an average of 6–7 years, despite advances in medical technology. (2) The death rate from prostate cancer has increased by 23 percent since 1973. (3) Oral cancer related to smoking occurs more than twice as often in men. (4) Three times more men than women suffer heart attacks before age 65. Nearly three in four coronary artery bypasses in 1995 were performed on men. (5) Bladder cancer occurs five times more often in men than women. (6) Nearly 95 percent of all DWI cases involve men. (7) According to the National Center for Health Statistics, in 1970, the suicide rate for white men was 9.4 per 100,000 as compared to 2.9 for white women. By 1986, the rate for white males had risen to 18.2 as compared to 4.1 for women, and by 1991, the rate for white male suicide was 19.3 per 100,000 as compared to a slight increase to 4.3 for women. In 1991, suicide rates for Black and Latino men were 11.5 per 100,000 or almost six times the rate of suicide for Black and Latino women, whose rate was 2 per 100,000. Suicide is the third leading cause of death among African American men. By 2001, suicide rates for all men had increased while suicide rates for men over 60 were 10–12 times higher than suicide rates for older women, with men over 85 having an astonishing suicide rate of 54 per 100,000 as compared to women in the same age group at 5 per 100,000 (Center for Disease Control, May 2004).

THE REASONS FOR MALE HEALTH PROBLEMS

The primary reasons for the health problems of men are as follows:

1. Men are more vulnerable to a range of health and mental health problems from birth. This vulnerability to health and behavioral problems continues throughout the life span. There is evidence that male vulnerability is both genetic and related to male socialization.

2. To maintain traditional notions of masculinity and because of reduced cognitive skills, poor judgment, and peer pressure, boys and young men are likely to engage in dangerous activities that

lead to physical disabilities and shortened life spans. This need to maintain traditional notions of masculinity may continue throughout the life span in some men. Men are far more prone to accidents and homicide than women. Tiller calls the need for men to prove themselves compensatory masculinity.

3. Men are less likely to seek help for physical and emotional problems than women. When they *do* seek help, it is usually at a more advanced stage in an illness or emotional problem. Many authors believe that the unwillingness to seek help for physical and emotional problems is explained by an unwillingness to feel vulnerable, passive, and out of control. If men feel vulnerable and passive when they receive medical care, perhaps part of the problem lies with the way care is given and men are treated by health professionals.

4. Men tend to internalize stress and convert it into physical problems, substance abuse, or emotional difficulty. To complicate this problem, men sometimes live lonely lives with no one to talk to, or they may find it difficult to communicate feelings with others.

5. Men often believe that being careful about health is a sign of weakness and that going to doctors may actually cause health problems. This belief often results in denial of bad health and failure to seek help before a condition becomes untreatable.

6. Heavy drinking is sometimes encouraged among men as a sign of masculinity. Popular sayings such as "drinking someone under the table" or that "He can sure handle his liquor" often reinforce men to drink too much or to binge drink. While drinking too much may not be a sign of addiction, it is dangerous behavior and may lead to sexual aggression, assaults, and accidents. Drinking as a sign of manliness is often reinforced by the popular culture, which romanticizes drinking and portrays it as an acceptable way for men to resolve personal problems.

WHAT LOVED ONES CAN DO TO IMPROVE THE HEALTH OF MEN IN THEIR LIVES

One of the things that loved ones can do to improve the health of men is to urge them to see a physician more often to evaluate health problems, but be aware that doctors are much less informative when it comes to providing preventative health information to men than when they work with women. Misener and Fuller (1995) report that only 29 percent of the physicians surveyed routinely provide instruction on performing testicular self-examination as compared to 86 percent of the physicians surveyed who provide instruction to women on performing breast self-examination.

To help reduce the risk of poor health and early death among men, Courtenay (2000) suggests the use of a health-risk assessment which includes physical and emotional indicators of potential health problems. Loved ones should be sensitive to these problems in evaluating how much at risk an individual may be. The potential factors that might indicate future health problems in men are as follows:

1. Satisfaction with work, personal life, and relationships.
2. Work-related problems including frequent job changes, fighting, or sexual harassment charges.
3. The date of the last health checkup and if any problems were noted.
4. How often a man sees a physician and under what circumstances.
5. Weight, amount of exercise, and caloric/fat intake.
6. Existence of serious health problems in a man's biological family.
7. Involvement in risky sports or recreation.
8. The number of times a man has been married or divorced.
9. Financial problems.
10. The average amount of alcohol or illicit drugs consumed per week.
11. All current prescription and over-the-counter drugs taken.
12. Indications of metabolic syndrome (high blood sugars, high blood pressure readings, waist size greater than 36, and high cholesterol, all of which are related to cardiovascular problems in men).
13. Sexual history including STDs, unprotected sex, number of sexual partners, recent sexual activity, erectile problems, or other sexual problems.
14. Last prostate checkup.
15. Smoking history.
16. Level of danger at work or the existence of dangerous chemicals in the workplace.
17. The length of the work commute.
18. The average number of hours of sleep per night.
19. Any history of violent behavior including fights and domestic violence.

20. Evidence of problems with temper and/or irritability.

21. Problems with depression and/or anxiety and any prior experiences and the reasons.

22. Early life health or emotional problems including fighting, abuse, gang membership, fire-setting, animal cruelty, and other problems that might suggest early life traumas and subsequent acting-out behavior or emotional problems.

23. Any history of accidents or brain injuries.

24. Any history of abusing children.

25. Prior surgeries or medical problems.

26. The number of close friends and how often a man sees them.

27. Attendance at church or synagogue.

28. Relationship with parents and how long parents lived or their current age if alive.

29. Educational level and achievement (grades).

One final reason for health problems in men is explained by a series of studies in which the level of self-involvement in health care correlated strongly with good health and longevity. The studies (Seligman 2004) show a very high relationship between self-involvement in one's own health care and the level of education. One study Seligman refers to is a 2001 study conducted by the CDC that found college graduates were "three times as likely to live healthy lives as those who never went beyond high school" (p. 114). With men increasingly opting out of higher education, the study predicts a high correlation between male health problems and the lack of self-involvement in their own health care. It further predicts that uninvolved patients will misuse what medical care they do get. According to Seligman, half of the 1.8 billion prescriptions issued annually are taken incorrectly and over 40 percent of the patients with diabetes (a large number of whom are men) don't understand blood sugars values or what to do if they are high. Seligman goes on to say:

Intelligent people tend to be the most knowledgeable about health related issues. Health literacy, matters more than it used to. In the past, big gains in health and longevity were associated with improvements in public sanitation, immunization and other initiatives not requiring decisions by ordinary citizens. But today, the major threats to health are chronic diseases—which, inescapably, require patients to participate in the treatment, which means in turn that they need to understand what's going on. (Seligman 2004, p. 114)

WHAT ALL OF THIS MEANS FOR OLDER MEN AND WOMEN

Those fellows at the Paella dinner are examples of men who have narrowly defined their roles. My guess is that outside of work they have very limited emotional ties to anyone or anything. They seemed miserable to me and it made me wonder how many older men in our society have so rigidly defined their roles that they can't enjoy the simple pleasures of life. It seems a shame because it must be a lonely existence to so narrowly define what's OK and what isn't, and it certainly can't be fun for the women, children, and friends in their lives. Hopefully this chapter about why some older men are that way will help both male and female readers better understand that men who rigidly define their roles in life without the possibility of change can inhibit happiness and relationships as they age. What women can do about it will be discussed in the next chapter on divorce and relationship breakups. Obviously, women want more than unemotional and rigid men in their lives or the high divorce rates that we see in couples over 50 wouldn't be happening.

MEN TALK ABOUT THEMSELVES IN A SUPPORT GROUP

Groups where men participate, including a number of alcohol- and drug-related treatment groups, are sometimes led by nonprofessionals and might best be thought of as self-help groups. In men's groups, participants are allowed to discuss emotional and often hidden issues that often match the experiences of other men. In one men's group for older men, a member talked about his father:

My father was a very sarcastic man with my brother, sister, mother and especially with me. He took pleasure in ridiculing us. He always seemed to know what really bothered us about ourselves and he could be deadly with his comments. He reserved for me, his oldest son, particular attention. When I started dating, he kept talking about my pimples, how I sometimes slouched, and how shy I was around girls. He said that I had a "nothing personality" and that girls would find me boring. These were all things that I worried about anyway and when he started talking about them, it made me more self-conscious than ever. He did this until I left home and once I was on my own, I let him have it back with the same meanness and condescension that he'd used with me. I knew his weaknesses and I was prepared to say anything that would hurt his feelings. It was complete role reversal. The more I criticized him, the more he praised me. What was this all about? In some strange way, I think he associated being critical with being loving. It got to a point as he aged where I couldn't stand the sight of him and I tried to avoid him as much as I could. Of course, he was very hurt. As he aged he seemed to just shrivel up like a dying bird, and when he passed away, he was almost invisible. I've hated myself for doing that to him, and I find that I've been depressed since he died last year.

Many of the men in the group had similar experiences with their own fathers and spoke about their feelings of guilt and recrimination at treating their fathers so badly after their fathers had done the same to them. One man in the group finally said:

You try your best to be a good person, even when people hurt you. As a way of trying to get healthy, all of us struck out at our fathers. I don't feel good about it but you learn from the experience and if you feel remorse now at what you did, it makes you a much better father with your own children. My father couldn't accept a truce and he went to his grave fighting with me. I regret it and I wish I could have changed things between us before he died, but you learn from those experiences and if a father wants to continue treating you with a great deal of meanness, you suck it up, make the best of it, and get on with your life. The thing is you don't have to believe what he says about you anymore. That's the difference between being a kid and being a grown up. You have control over your feelings now because you know a lot more about yourself.

Another member of the group said:

My father was abusive, an alcoholic, and a very mean drunk. When my mom died he came to live with me and my wife and kids. I hated him and treated him very badly. It embarrassed my kids the way I was acting, and we had a family meeting where they told me how they felt. They said it was affecting my relationship with them. So we had another family meeting with the old man present and we talked a lot of things through. The fact is that my father has changed over the years and he's become a very decent person. I can't forgive him for what he did when I was growing up but I'm being much better with him and the kids comment about how nice it is to have a peaceful family again.

These types of exchanges typify men's groups and have a particularly positive impact on the way men see themselves and the way they problem-solve common life issues. Getting feedback from other men often has a powerful impact. As another member of the group said:

When I heard about this group, I thought it was a lot of crap. It wasn't even led by a therapist, just a bunch of guys shooting the breeze. I thought it would be like the women's groups I'd heard about where they whine, and complain, and nothing ever changes. But this group has had a really big effect on me. I trust everyone and I feel safe saying what I say. We respect each other's privacy and we don't get real confrontational, even when guys are starting to lose it. What we do is listen, sympathize sometimes, give advice and a lot of support. We feel comfortable accepting the advice or turning it down, and we feel OK about not talking when it feels right to keep quiet. I really care about these guys.

It was interesting to see how long it took us to talk about real stuff instead of being phony. Once we got past that point, the spigot opened and we were talking about some pretty heavy stuff: impotence, attraction to other women than our wives, drinking, our feelings about gays, the kids we have who don't like us much, working, just a lot of things. I wouldn't say it's like therapy. It's more like a bunch of guys being honest with each other. It doesn't happen often that men are honest with other men, but when it does, it's pretty powerful.

SUMMARY

This chapter explains the relationship problems of men and why women have such difficulty dealing with some of the men in their lives. Men and women have different genetic makeups, and their life experience teach them different lessons. Understanding men and how to approach relationship issues can be a positive way of resolving problems women readers may have with the men in their lives.

REFERENCES

Bereska, T. M. (January 31, 2003). "The Changing Boys' World in the 20th Century: Reality and Fiction." *Journal of Men's Studies* 11 (2): 157–83.

Brannon, R. C. (1976). "No 'Sissy Stuff': The Stigma of Anything Vaguely Feminine." In S. Sailid and R. Brannon (eds.), *The Forty-Nine Percent Majority*. Reading, MA: Addison-Wesley: 57–87.

Brooks, G. R. (1990). "Traditional Men in Marital Therapy." *Journal of Feminist Family Therapy* 2 (3/4): 51–65.

Courtenay, W. H. (2000). "Behavioral Factors Associated with Disease, Injury, and Death among Men: Evidence and Implications for Prevention." *Journal of Men's Studies* 9 (1): 81–104.

Cowley, G. (June 16, 2003). "Why We Strive for Status." *Newsweek* 67–70.

Drug Store News (July 20, 1998). "Men's Health at a Glance: A Fact Sheet for Pharmacists." Retrieved May 17, 2004 from: http://www.findarticles .com/cf_0/m3374/n11_v20/20969541/p1/article.jhtml?term=men+%2B +health.

Epperly, T. D., and Moore, K. E. (July 1, 2000). "Health Issues in Men Part II: Common Psychosocial Disorders." *American Family Physician*. Retrieved from: http://www.findarticles.com/cf_0/m3225/1_62/65864000/ print.jhtml.

Fabes, R. A., Eisenberg, N., Karbon, M., Troyer, D., and Switzer, G. (1994). "The Relation of Children's Emotion Regulation to Their Vicarious Emotional Responses and Comforting Behaviors." *Child Development* 65: 1678–93.

Fivush, R. (1989). "Exploring Sex Differences in the Emotional Content of Mother-Child Conversations about the Past." *Sex Roles: A Journal of Research* 20: 675–91.

Gilligan, C. (1982). *In a Different Voice*. Cambridge, MA: Harvard University Press.

Glicken, M. D. (2005). *Ending the Sex Wars: A Woman's Guide to Understanding Men*. Lincoln, NE: iUniverse.

Gupta, S. (May 12, 2003). "Why Men Die Young." *Time* 161 (19): 84.

Harrison, J., Chin, J., and Ficarrotto, T. (1988). "Warning: Masculinity May Be Dangerous to Your Health." In M. S. Kimmel and M. A. Messner (eds.), *Men's Lives*. New York: MacMillan: 271–85.

Hopkins, W. D., and Bard, K. A. (1993). "Hemispheric Specialisation in Infant Chimpanzees (Pan troglodytes): Evidence for a Relation with Gender and Arousal." *Developmental Psychobiology* 26: 219–35.

Keller, A. K., and West, M. (1995). "Attachment Organisation and Vulner-ability to Loss, Separation, and Abuse in Disturbed Adolescents." In Goldberg, S., Muir, R., and Kerr, J. (eds.), *Attachment Theory: Social, Developmental and Clinical Perspectives*. Hillsdale, NJ: Analytic Press: 327.

Kohlberg, L. (1987). *Child Psychology and Childhood Education: A Cognitive Developmental View*. Long Group United Kingdom: London.

Kraemer, S. (2000). "The Fragile Male." *British Medical Journal* 321: 1609–12.

Levinson, D. J., Darrow, C. N., Klein, E. B., Levinson, M. H., and McGee, B. (1978). *The Seasons of a Man's Life*. New York: Ballantine Books.

Mahalik, J. R., Locke, B. D., Theodore, H., Cournoyer, R. J., and Lloyd, B. F. (2001). A Cross-National and Cross-Sectional Comparison of Men's Gender Role Conflict and Its Relationship to Social Intimacy and Self-Esteem." *Sex Roles* 43: 40–57. Retrieved May 26, 2004 from: www.findarticles.com/cf_0/PI/search.jhtml?key=men%27s+health&page=3&magR=all+magazines.

Mead, M. (1935). *Sex and Temperament in Three Primitive Societies*. New York: William Morrow and Co.

Misener, T. R., and Fuller, S. G. (1995). "Testicular Versus Breast and Colorectal Cancer Screen: Early Detection Practices of Primary Care Physicians." *Cancer Practice* 3 (5): 310–16.

Murray, L., Kempton, C., Woolgar, M., and Hooper, R. (1993). "Depressed Mothers' Speech to Their Infants and Its Relation to Infant Gender and Cognitive Development." *Journal of Child Psychiatry* 34: 1083–101.

National Center for Chronic Disease Prevention and Health (2001). Suicide Facts and Statistics. Retrieved May 12, 2004 from: http://www.nimh.nih.gov/suicideprevention/suifact.cfm.

O'Neil, J. M. (1981). "Patterns of Gender Role Conflict: Sexism and Fear of Femininity in Men's Lives." *Personnel and Guidance Journal* 60.

O'Neil, J. M., and Egan, J. (1992). "Men's Gender Role Transitions Over the Life Span: Transformations and Fears of Femininity." *Journal of Mental Health Counseling* 14: 305–24.

Parker, J. D. A., Keightley, M. L., Smith, C. T., and Taylor, G. (1999). "Interhemispheric Transfer Deficit in Alexithymia: An Experimental Study." *Psychosomatic Medicine* 61: 464–68.

Pitman, F. S. (1993). *Man Enough: Fathers, Sons, and the Search for Masculinity*. New York: Putnam Publishing Group.

Pleck, J. H. (1980). Men's Power with Women, Other Men, and Society: A Men's Movement Analysis. In Pleck, E., and Pleck, J. H. (eds.), *The American Man*. Englewood Cliffs, NJ: Prentice Hall: 417–33.

——— (1987). "The Contemporary Man." In Scher, M., Good, M. S. G., and Eichenfield, G. A. (eds). *Handbook of Counseling & Psychotherapy with Men*. Newbury Park, CA: Sage: 16–27.

———— (1995). "The Gender Role Strain Paradigm: An Update." In Levant, R. F., and Pollack, W. S. (eds.), *A New Psychology of Men*. New York: Basic Books: 11–32.

Reuben, D. B., Yoshikawa, T. T., and Besdine, R. W., eds. (1996). *Geriatrics Review Syllabus: A Core Curriculum in Geriatric Medicine* (3rd ed.). New York: American Geriatric Society: 207–10.

Robertson, J., and Fitzgerald, L. (April 1992). "Overcoming the Masculine Mystique: Preferences for Alternative Forms of Assistance among Men Who Avoid Counseling." *Journal of Counseling Psychology* 39 (2): 240–46.

Rout, U. (1999). "Gender Differences in Stress, Satisfaction, and Mental Wellbeing among General Practitioners in England. *Psychological Health Medicine* 4: 345–54.

Sackett, G. P. (1972). "Exploratory Behavior of Rhesus Monkeys as a Function of Rearing Experiences and Sex." *Developmental Psychology* 6: 260–70.

Sargent, J. (1999). "Review of William Pollack, Ph.D. Random House, New York, 1998, 450 pages." *Everyman: A Men's Journal* no. 36: 45.

Scher, M. (January 1979). "On Counseling Men." *Personnel and Guidance Journal*: 252–54.

———— (Fall 1990). "Effect of Gender Role Incongruencies on Men's Experiences as Clients in Psychotherapy." *Psychotherapy* 27: 322–26.

Seligman, D. (June 7, 2004). "Why the Rich Live Longer." *Forbes* 173 (12): 113–14.

Spielberg, W. E. (1993). "Why Men Need to Be Heroic." *Journal of Men's Studies* 2 (2): 173–78.

Van Wormer, K. (1999). "The Strengths Perspective: A Paradigm for Correctional Counseling." *Federal Probation* 63 (1): 51–58.

Wade, J. C., and Brittan-Powell, C. (September 2000). "Male Reference Group Identity Dependence: Support for Construct Validity." *Sex Roles* 12 (5): 45–63. Retrieved June 17, 2004 from: http://www.findarticles .com/cf_0/m2294/2000_Sept/71118810/p1/article.jhtml?term=men+%2B +Counseling.

Wilson, J. Q. (1993). "On Gender." *Public Interest* no. 112: 3–27.

Worell, J. (1981). "Life-Span Sex Roles: Development, Continuity, and Change." In Lerner, R. M., and Busch-Rossnagel, N. A. (eds.), *Individuals as Producers of Their Development: A Life-Span Perspective*. New York: Academic Press: 37–71.

Yacovene, D. (1990). "Abolitionists and the 'Language of Fraternal Love.'" In Carnes, M. C., and Griffen, C. (eds.), *Meanings for Manhood: Constructions of Masculinity in Victorian America*. Chicago: University of Chicago Press: 85–95.

Zaslow, M. J., and Hayes, C. D. (1986). "Sex Differences in Children's Response to Psychosocial Stress: Toward a Cross-context Analysis." In Lamb, M. E., Brown, A. L., and Rogoff, B. (eds.), *Advances in Developmental Psychology Vol 4*. Hillsdale, NJ: Erlbaum: 285–337.

CHAPTER 4
Enjoying Older Adult Sexuality

INTRODUCTION

This chapter deals with issues of intimacy. As the following discussion indicates, age is no barrier to having a long and enjoyable love life. Older adults continue to be sexually active in frequency that may surprise many of you. Stein (2007) found that in his study of 3,000 U.S. adults ages 57–85, half to three-quarters of the respondents remained sexually active, with a "significant population engaging in frequent and varied sex" (p. A1). The study indicates, not surprisingly, that healthier people reported the highest rates of sexual activity and that a healthy sex life may itself help keep people vibrant. According to Stein the study found that 28 percent of the men and 14 percent of the women said sex was very important, and those with partners reported being as sexually active as adults in their forties and fifties. "But even among the oldest age group (80–85), 54% of those who were sexually active reported having sex at least two to three times per month, and 23% reported having sex once a week or more" (p. A1).

When Stein broke the data down by age, he found that in the preceding 12 months, 73 percent of those ages 57–64, 53 percent of those ages 65–74, and 26 percent of those ages 75–85 said they were sexually active. Among those reporting good or excellent health, 81 percent of men and 51 percent of women said they had been sexually active in the past year.

Reporting on numerous studies of sexual health in older adults, Nuzzo (2008) writes, "If we manage to stay happy, healthy and socially connected as we get older—a tall order but not impossible—chances are good that we can continue to enjoy sex as long as we desire" (p. 1).

In a National Council on the Aging study (1998), the following data were found:

o 48% of men and women over 60 are sexually active (some form of sexual activity once a month).

o 39% of men and women over 60 would like to be more active than they are.

o About 75% of sexually active older Americans say their sex life today is as emotionally satisfying or even more satisfying than it was when they were in their forties.

Data for women over 60 were as follows:

o 37% are sexually active.

o 62% say sex is better, or at least equally as physically satisfying, as it was at 40.

o Women who are not sexually active often give lack of a partner as the reason.

o 69% say sex is equally as emotionally satisfying as it was at 40.

o 47% say sex is important to a relationship.

Data for men over 60 were as follows:

o 61% are sexually active.

o 61% say sex is better, or at least equally as physically satisfying as it was at 40.

o 76% say sex is equally as emotionally satisfying as it was at 40.

o 72% say sex is important to a relationship.

PHYSICAL AND EMOTIONAL PROBLEMS THAT AFFECT INTIMACY

As we age we may experience health problems that sometimes affect our sexual behavior. They can be an annoyance, but if you are willing to try a range of activities that might satisfy you and your mate, there is no reason you can't have a satisfying sex life for as long as you want. Many people continue to be sexually active even if they have health problems or experience a sexual problem. Stein (2007) found that even though about half of the people in his study reported at least one sexual problem, they still remained sexually active. The most common problems reported were erectile problems in men (37% of the men in the study) and vaginal dryness in women (39% in the study). Neither problem is a reason to avoid sex.

PHYSICAL REASONS FOR SEXUAL PROBLEMS IN MEN

Many of the erectile problems in men are caused by a lack of being sexually stimulated. This happens when men are tired, not aroused, or when they've been drinking. Certain medications can have an impact on having an erection. It's always wise to consider the logical reasons for not having an erection before becoming anxious about it. The fact is that men of all ages have problems getting erections when they are anxious, tired, intoxicated, or not aroused. Even drugs like Viagra don't work unless you're aroused. So, male readers, if you're concerned about a physical reason for erectile problems, remember that men have erections about every 90 minutes while asleep. If you have a partner, ask them to check to see if this is happening. If it isn't happening the most likely culprit is medication for blood pressure problems, diabetes, or in some instances, spinal problems. The good news is that only about 10 percent of the reasons for erectile problems are physical. Do we lose some of our ability to maintain an erection as we age? Yes, but that doesn't mean that you can't be stimulated repeatedly by a partner during sexual activity to maintain an erection for intercourse.

The words used to describe problems men have in getting an erection when they're having sex for the first time with a new partner are "performance anxiety." It's common in every man at every age so if it happens to you, don't worry about it. It's normal. It's difficult to have an erection when you're thinking about it or if you're worried you won't have one. Another common problem men of all ages have is premature ejaculation, or having an orgasm as you begin to enter your partner. If there is a man alive who hasn't had a premature ejaculation, step forward and I'll buy you dinner. Most of us learn that once we have an erection we have to focus our thoughts on other issues or we'll immediately have an orgasm. It takes some practice, and sometimes when we've been erect for a long time it may be hard to ejaculate. If that's a problem, oral sex or gentle rubbing of the penis by your partner using a lubricant can often help. The important thing to remember is not to make a big deal out of it. If your wife or partner *does* make a big deal out of it, you need to have a frank discussion with her. Just as women aren't always able to be aroused or have an orgasm, the same thing happens to men. It's just part of the human experience.

PHYSICAL REASONS FOR SEXUAL PROBLEMS IN WOMEN

Older women sometimes experience vaginal dryness even when they are aroused. It's a normal part of the sexual experience and it happens to most women at some time or another. There are many lubricants on the market that can make this problem go away quickly. The more common reason for vaginal dryness is lack of arousal. Your mate may not provide sufficient foreplay to arouse you, or the foreplay itself may not be arousing. You need to help your partner by giving loving suggestions. Oral sex can be very stimulating to many women. So can gentle touch to the vaginal area. Should a woman have an orgasm every time she has sex? Of course not. Like men, you need to be aroused and in the mood, and enough time has to pass for the orgasm to happen. Some men get very upset if you don't have an orgasm every time you have sex. It's important not to make a big deal out of it, but just as men don't always have an orgasm, neither do women.

The common reasons for female sexual problems are similar to those of men. Medication reduces sexual desire in 44 percent of men and 16 percent of women. Medical conditions reduce desire for sex. Negative feelings or anger at a spouse often reduce desire for sex, as does lack of physical attraction to a partner. A case study in this chapter describes an older couple in which the husband began losing his desire for his wife and how it was dealt with in counseling.

PSYCHOLOGICAL CHANGES IN MEN AND WOMEN AS THEY AGE

Often the same sexual problems that affect men and women earlier in life affect them as they age. Feeling embarrassed or ashamed about sexual needs and performance anxiety may affect a person's ability to become aroused. Changes in appearance might also affect the ability to emotionally and physically connect with a partner. A poor body image may reduce sex drive because one of the partners no longer feels worthy of sexual attention from the other partner. The stress of worrying too much about how one will perform can trigger impotence in men or a lack of arousal in women. Taking things slowly and being patient can help reduce performance anxiety—the main cause of sexual difficulties in the young and the old.

A University of Missouri at Kansas City report (2007) indicates that the following emotional factors may result in sexual problems for older adults: (1) Sexual activity in middle age is a strong predictor of sexual activity in old age; (2) negative attitudes about sexual activities other than intercourse, such as oral sex, may interfere with an openness to try new ways of expressing intimacy; (3) reactions and beliefs about physiological changes or illness-induced changes may have a negative impact on sexual functioning; (4) reactions to the attitudes of others, society, or adult children often have a powerful impact on self-concept and may affect sexual behavior; and (5) living arrangements that do not allow for privacy, such as long-term care facilities, create a barrier to sexual activity.

SUGGESTIONS FOR IMPROVING OLDER ADULT INTIMACY

1. Expand your definition of sex to include touch, sensual massage, masturbation, and oral sex.

2. Improve your communications with your partner. When sexual problems exist it can be helpful for partners to discuss physical or emotional changes they may be going through, and what partners can do to accommodate those changes during intimacy. Communication itself can be arousing.

3. Make changes in your sexual routines. Simple changes can improve your love life, including changing the time of day when you have sex to a time when both partners have the most energy (for example, mornings, when a couple has just had a refreshing night of sleep). Because it might take longer to become aroused, couples might take more time to set the stage for romance, such as a romantic dinner or an evening of dancing.

4. Caring for one's health. Older couples need to have healthy diets and regular exercise to keep their bodies fit, since this keeps a person ready for sex at any age. Couples should also avoid alcohol before having sex because it often decreases sexual functioning in both men and women. Illegal drugs such as marijuana and cocaine impair sexual functioning, as do a number of prescription drugs.

Couples on medication should ask their doctors or pharmacists about sexual side effects. There are also a number of Web sites about medication that discuss side effects. If a medication has a sexual side effect, perhaps other medications with less adverse effects might be used.

A CASE STUDY: LOSING SEXUAL INTEREST IN A PARTNER

The following case study (Glicken 2009, 132–34) appeared in a book I wrote for mental health professionals working with an aging population experiencing social and emotional problems. The author thanks Elsevier, Inc. for permission to use it in this book.

The following case involves a 67-year-old male and a female 64-year-old who have been married for 35 years and are the parents of three grown and successful children. The wife tells the first part of the story, followed by the husband.

Her Story: "We've been married over 35 years and have what I think is an exceptional life by any measure. We have good friends, loving children, and we're financially in very good shape. Jack started losing interest in having sex with me two years ago. When I asked why our sex life wasn't as good as it used to be (we'd previously had sex at least three times a week), he said that he just didn't have much of a sex drive, yet I caught him masturbating at the computer on one of those porn sites. I didn't say anything, but I know he goes into those sites once or twice a day. It's hurtful to me that he masturbates instead of having sex with me, but I can't get up the courage to discuss it. He seems happy with me otherwise, but I miss sex and I'm feeling pretty rejected."

His Story: "I love my wife but the truth is that I don't find her attractive anymore. She's put on a lot of weight and she looks old to me. She's losing her hair and when I see her naked it repulses me. After 35 years together the passion isn't what it used to be but this is much more serious, I think. The thought of having sex with her makes me physically ill and a couple of times, during oral sex, I've gotten so ill I've vomited. I masturbate while looking at porno sites. It seems a harmless way to deal with my sexual needs, but my guess is that Jackie knows and resents it. I can't get myself to talk to her about it since I think it would break her heart, and anyway, it makes me feel like a complete ass."

Professional Help: The counselor who ultimately saw this couple did so for the purpose of divorce mediation since Jackie, much against her true wishes but because of deeply hurt feelings, initiated divorce proceedings against Jack. The counselor, a licensed and highly experienced clinical social worker, quickly realized that neither partner wanted a divorce, but that the sexual problem was serious. Jack had no desire to have sex with other women and felt fine masturbating to porno sites. Jackie found that an unacceptable solution. The social worker asked the couple to discuss their sexual problem. Jack said, "You've put on at least 100 pounds since we married. You don't dress up or put on makeup the way you used to. You wear old lady clothes, and you never try and look nice for me. Your sleep apnea, which the doctor said was due to your weight, requires that you wear a breathing mask at night. How appealing do you think that is for me?"

Jackie responded by saying, "If I lost weight and started to look better would that even make a difference? Much of the weight I've put on happened in the past couple of years when you clearly didn't want to have sex with me. And when this all started, I was dressing up and I looked good but you stopped having interest in me anyway, so stop putting the blame for your problem on me. You just find those bimbos on the Internet a lot sexier than a 64-year-old woman—any 64-year-old woman. Admit it."

Jack told Jackie, "Maybe that's true. Maybe young women turn me on, but we have a relationship I treasure. I've never been unfaithful, I still love you. You want to break up a marriage because after 35 years we don't have a sex life? That seems pretty extreme to me. Do you think you'll go out there in the world and a prince charming who wants to have sex with you all the time will come along?"

"No," Jackie replied, "no I don't, but I won't have to live with the humiliation of sleeping with a man who doesn't want to touch me, will I."

In further discussions Jackie agreed to lose weight and begin taking better care of herself. She joined a tennis club, began working out, and went to people who would help her choose more attractive clothing and better makeup. Jack agreed to stop using porn sites and to stop masturbating. As Jack's sexual needs increased and Jackie began looking better, the sex life they enjoyed earlier slowly began to return. The counselor who worked with them said:

> You see a lot of older adults like Jack and Jackie who still love one another but the passion is gone and it's hurtful. Many of them describe their partners as roommates or business partners. I know that sexual distance often develops when partners begin to find

one another unattractive. I also felt that with Jack not mastur bating he would pay more attention to Jackie to have his sexual needs met if Jackie did something to improve her attractiveness to Jack. She readily agreed to lose weight since she felt uncomfortable and unattractive at her current weight. Joining a weight loss program and the tennis club helped her lose weight and improve her self-esteem. She also began to discover that, as she lost weight and dressed more attractively that men in her age group began to look at her in ways they hadn't in awhile. Jack also noticed which helped improve the frequency of sexual contact. Feeling a bit worried that someone might take Jackie away from him increased his desire to please her. It's not an ideal solution since you would hope that love, mutual concern, and the desire to please one another would resolve this problem naturally without the need for a professional. In my experience sex is a difficult thing for people to talk about to one another. Sometimes simple solutions such as this one are called for. We still don't know a lot about older sexuality and few older adults seek help when they have sexual problems, believing that it's all about aging and nothing can be done to help. Perhaps as the number of older men and women increases and a new openness develops as people live longer, more older adults will seek help. Certainly doctors, who more often work with older adults than mental health professionals can help matters by discussing sexual problems and, when appropriate, referring people for counseling. My experience is that older adults work hard to improve emotional difficulties and that sexual problems are often easier to resolve with older people than with young adults. I think it's because older people want to get on with life in the easiest way they can and holding on to problems just seems like a waste of time.

SUMMARY

This chapter explores the issues of love and intimacy in older adulthood. Data are provided showing that many older adults maintain robust sexual lives. Physical and emotional issues that may interfere with love and intimacy are provided, along with a case study exploring an older couple whose love life has become troublesome with a counseling intervention included.

REFERENCES

Bancroft, J. H. J. (2007). "Sex and Aging." http://cas.umkc.edu/casww/sa/ Sex.htm.

Clinical Effectiveness Group, for The Association of Genitourinary Medicine and Medical Society of the Study of Venereal Diseases (2005). National Guidelines for the Management of the Viral Hepatitides A, B and C. http://www.bashh.org/guidelines.

Erikson, E. H. (1963). *Childhood and Society* (2nd ed.). New York: Norton.

Genevay, B. (1999). "Intimacy and Older People: Much More than Sex." *Dimensions* 6 (3).

Huffstetler, B. (Spring 2006) "Sexuality in Older Adults: A Deconstructionist Perspective." *ADUITSPAN* 5 (1): 4–14.

Kaas, M. J. (1981). "Geriatric Sexuality Breakdown Syndrome." *International Journal of Aging and Human Development* 13: 71–77.

The National Council on the Aging (September 1998). *Healthy Sexuality and Vital Aging. Executive Summary*: 1–3.

Nuzzo, R. (November 17, 2008). "Sexual Health in Older Adults." Retrieved February 6, 2009 from: http://www.latimes.com/features/health/la-he -mating17-2008nov17,0,1501668.story.

Perman, D. (February 2, 2006). "The Changing Face of Romance in 2006: Are Valentines Just for the Young?" *Intimacy and Aging: Tips for Sexual Health and Happiness. UBC Reports* 52 (2).

Stein, R. (August 23, 2007). "Elderly Staying Sexually Active." *Washington Post*. http://www.washingtonpost.com/wp-dyn/content/article/2007/ 08/22/AR2007082202000_pf.html.

Walsh, F. (1988). "The Family in Later Life." In Carter, B., and McGoldrick, M. (eds.), *The Changing Family Life Cycle* (2nd ed.). New York: Gardner: 311–32.

Zernike, K. (November 18, 2007). "Still Many-Splendored: Love in the Time of Dementia." *New York Times*. http://www.nytimes.com/2007/11/18/ weekinreview/18zernike.html.

CHAPTER 5

Coping with Later-Life Divorces and Breakups

INTRODUCTION

Ending a long-term relationship is hurtful at any age, but it's particularly hurtful as we get older. A feeling of having been used often accompanies an even stronger feeling that no one will find us attractive now, and that we'll be alone and without intimacy for the rest of our lives. Both feelings influence how we adjust to single life and how we fashion a strategy to seek companionship and a suitable mate.

More older people than ever are getting divorced. According to the U.S. Census Bureau, 28.6 percent of adults ages 45–59 were unattached in 2003, compared with only 18.8 percent in 1980. Of those, 16.6 percent were divorced, 2.9 percent were widowed, and 9.1 percent had never been married. Clarke (1995) reports that divorce rates for adults 65 and over have steadily increased since 1980. Shapiro (2003) believes that as increasing numbers of older adults divorce and are essentially living alone and that the increased burden for care as people age will be shared by society and, more specifically by children, creating additional tension between parents and children. According to Uhlenberg and colleagues (1990), mid- to later-life divorce have been estimated to account for 25 percent or more of all divorces in the United States.

WHY LATER-LIFE DIVORCES ARE INCREASING

In a troubling article on marriage by Tsing Loh (2009) called "On Marriage: Let's Call the Whole Thing Off," the author argues that many people get very little out of marriage as they age. Relationships, which were once so vibrant, become sexless and businesslike as partners spend increasing amounts of time dealing with the rearing of children and the stressors and rewards of work and their personal lives. She believes that a primary reason American marriages so often end in divorce is that people begin to ask themselves if they're getting anything out of the relationship other than the hard work of raising children and maintaining a home, much of which falls on the shoulders of women. She also believes that while Americans believe in marriage more than almost any other national group, we have an independent streak that bodes badly for long-term relationships.

Writing about her own divorce she asks why should she keep a marriage alive after it's been dead for years, and writes,

> Given my staggering working mother's to-do list, I cannot take on yet another arduous home- and self-improvement project, that of rekindling our romance. Sobered by this failure as a mother ... I've begun to wonder, what with all the abject and swallowed misery: Why do we still insist on marriage? Sure, it made sense to agrarian families before 1900, when to farm the land one needed two spouses, grandparents, and a raft of children. But now that we have white-collar work and washing machines, and our life expectancy has shot from 47 to 77, isn't the idea of lifelong marriage obsolete? (p. 1)

The author goes on to say that many people who study marriage believe that marriage and long-term relationships are biologically meant to last about four years, or the length of time it takes to get one child through infancy. There is also the matter of the type of personality we possess and how that works out with a partner. Fischer (2009) believes there are four basic personality types:

1. **The Explorer.** The libidinous, creative adventurer who acts "on the spur of the moment."
2. **The Builder.** The much calmer person who has "traditional values." The Builder also "would rather have loyal friends than interesting friends," enjoys routines, and places a high priority on taking care of his or her possessions.
3. **The Director.** The "analytical and logical" thinker who enjoys a good argument. The Director wants to discover all the features of his or her new camera or computer.

4. **The Negotiator.** The touchy-feely communicator who imagines "both wonderful and horrible things happening" to him- or herself.

SUCCESSFUL MATCHES

Fischer (2009) suggests that the following matches are often more successful in long-term relationships. Remember that this doesn't always hold true since we all know couples who seem very ill-suited for one another but who have great marriages.

1. **Explorer/Explorer.** Explorers are attracted to other Explorers because they crave excitement; they want optimism, impulsivity, and curiosity in their partner. The Explorer/Explorer match is generally strong because Explorers love adventure and want a partner to share their spontaneity. But this match can have problems. Since both are willing to tolerate risks, two Explorers can find themselves in disastrous situations. And Explorers are not usually very introspective, so the pair often avoids difficult discussions.

2. **Builder/Builder.** Like Explorers, Builders are attracted to each other. They are most likely to marry each other and to say they are happy in their marriage and less likely to divorce than other combinations. Builders like bringing people and community together and enjoy working together. They are successful at building large circles of close friends and making sensible decisions about money, family, and feelings together and value security above almost everything else.

3. **Director/Negotiator.** Unlike Builders and Explorers, who are often attracted to people of their own type, Directors and Negotiators are often drawn to each other. They complement each other, as Negotiators see the big picture while Directors focus on smaller pieces of the puzzle. Negotiators are skilled at seeing all angles without taking action and Directors are decisive yet often don't analyze the data well. The two types are also compatible socially. Negotiators are good at smoothing over Directors' inappropriate comments, and Directors admire the diplomatic nature of Negotiators.

Tsing Loh ends her article with the depressing statement that we should avoid marriage altogether or "suffer the emotional pain, the humiliation, and the logistical difficulty, not to mention the expense, of breaking up a long-term union at midlife for something as demonstrably fleeting as love" (p. 1). Most of what is done in marriage, she argues, can be done by single people with support systems or open marriages where two people share expenses and childrearing but seek intimacy elsewhere in a mature way.

What this has to do with older marriages is that over time, the stress and lack of passion in a marriage begins to affect the underlying reasons to stay in a marriage: love and loyalty. As children leave home and childrearing stops being a primary reason to stay in an unhappy marriage, many older men and women can no longer justify remaining in a marriage and divorce often follows. Many of these marriages have lasted 30 or more years but began having problems far earlier. When they end, it is often with sadness but not rancor, since both partners often feel relieved. This doesn't negate the disruption in lives or many of the difficulties in adjusting to single life. It simply means that when love and passion end, the relief people feel often outweighs the stress and sadness of maintaining a badly functioning marriage. As Loh concludes, "To work, to parent, to housekeep, to be the ones who schedule 'date night,' only to be reprimanded in the home by husbands, and then, in the bedroom, to be ignored—it's a bum deal. And while our women's magazines exhort us to rekindle the romance, you rarely see men's magazines exhorting men to rekindle the romance." That, from a woman in her late forties, seems to me to be the kind of eroding feeling about marriage that ultimately starts the older marriage decline and contributes to the increased later-life divorced rate.

Is marriage something that one can approach scientifically? People such as Fischer believe that there are biochemical and personality components of people that bode well or badly for long-term relationships. But as many of us know, people can change, and we can change as well. What begins as a promising relationship may erode over time for many reasons that are neither biochemical nor related to the brain. Illness, money worries, children with traumatic physical problems, loss of work, and changes in how attracted we are to our partners as they age often contribute to whether relationships last. And while Americans strongly believe in marriage, we also have an independent streak and a belief that we have the ability to change our level of happiness by finding new jobs, new places to live and, in many cases, new husbands, wives, and lovers.

SOME COMMON MYTHS ABOUT DIVORCE

Popenoe (2009) suggests the following myths about divorce:

1. **Second Marriages. Question (Q):** Because people learn from their bad experiences, don't second marriages tend to be more successful than first marriages? **Answer (A):** Although many people who divorce have successful subsequent marriages, the divorce rate of remarriages is in fact higher than that of first marriages (Goldstein 1999).

2. **Living Together. Q:** Is living together before marriage a good way to reduce the chances of eventually divorcing? **A:** Many studies have found that those who live together before marriage have a considerably *higher* chance of eventually divorcing. The reasons for this are not well understood. In part, people who are willing to cohabit may also be those who are more willing to divorce. There is some evidence that the act of cohabitation itself generates attitudes in people that are more conducive to divorce including the attitude that relationships are temporary and can easily be ended (DeMaris and Rao 1992).

3. **Finances. Q:** Following divorce, doesn't the woman's standard of living plummet by 73 percent while that of the man improves by 42 percent? **A:** This dramatic inequity, one of the most widely publicized statistics from the social sciences, was later found to be based on a faulty calculation. A reanalysis of the data determined that the woman's loss was 27 percent while the man's gain was 10 percent. Irrespective of the magnitude of the differences, the gender gap is real and seems not to have narrowed much in recent decades (Smock 1993).

4. **Children. Q:** When parents don't get along, aren't children better off if their parents divorce than if they stay together? **A:** A recent large-scale, long-term study suggests otherwise. While it found that parents' marital unhappiness and discord have a broad negative impact on virtually every dimension of their children's well-being, so does going through a divorce. In examining the negative impacts on children more closely, the study discovered that it was only the children in very high-conflict homes who benefited from the conflict removal that divorce may bring. In lower-conflict marriages that end in divorce—and the study found that perhaps as many as two-thirds of the divorces were of

this type—the situation of the children was made much worse following a divorce. Based on the findings of this study, therefore, except in the minority of high-conflict marriages, it is better for the children if their parents stay together and work out their problems than if they divorce (Amato and Booth 1997).

5. **Unhappiness. Q:** Isn't being very unhappy at certain points in a marriage a good sign that the marriage will eventually end in divorce? **A:** All marriages have their ups and downs. Recent research using a large national sample found that 86 percent of people who were unhappily married in the late 1980s and stayed with the marriage indicated when interviewed five years later that they were happier. Indeed, three-fifths of the formerly unhappily married couples rated their marriages as either "very happy" or "quite happy" (Waite 2000).

6. **Who Initiates Divorce? Q:** Isn't it usually men who initiate divorce proceedings? **A:** Two-thirds of all divorces are initiated by women. One recent study found that many of the reasons for this have to do with the nature of our divorce laws. For example, in most states women have a good chance of receiving custody of their children. Because women more strongly want to keep their children with them, in states where there is a presumption of shared custody with the husband the percentage of women who initiate divorces is much lower. Also, the higher rate of women initiators is probably due to the fact that men are more likely to have "badly behaved." Husbands, for example, are more likely than wives to have problems with drinking, drug abuse, and infidelity (Brinig and Allen, 2000).

THE IMPACT OF LATER-LIFE DIVORCE

Anyone who has gone through a divorce or the breakup of a long-term relationship knows that it is hurtful. But for older adults it is particularly hurtful. An AARP Study (2004) of divorced men and women in their fifties, sixties, and seventies found that "Compared to other losses that may occur at midlife or older, people age 40 and older generally feel that divorce is more emotionally devastating than losing a job, about equal to experiencing a major illness, and somewhat less devastating than a spouse's death" (p. 1).

In addition to emotional turmoil, the AARP study reported that 40 percent of the divorced men and women in the study worried about what lay ahead in their lives, 29 percent suffered from loneliness or depression, 25 percent felt deserted or betrayed, 23 percent felt unloved, and 20 percent simply felt inadequate. People in the study also faced many fears including the fear of being alone (45%), the fear of failing again if they remarried (31%), the fear of being financially destitute (28%), concerns about never finding anyone to marry or live with (24%), and worries about staying angry and bitter for a long period of time (20%). Sixteen percent worried that they would stay depressed, and 14 percent worried that they would never see their children again. You might argue that the majority of people in the study didn't have worries or fears, but these numbers are very large and indicate that divorce is an emotionally troubling experience for many older people.

The study also found that women initiate a divorce more often than men even though divorce will leave them more financially vulnerable. They do this because they blame their husbands for failed marriages, particularly when abuse is present. Even so, the divorce often came as a surprise to men in the study.

Despite the many concerns divorced women have when they discuss the impact of divorce, women seem to cope better than men. According to the study, "The majority [of women] feel they are on the top rungs of the ladder of life. Their outlook is on a par with that of the general population age 45 or older, and better than that of singles ages 40 to 69. Those who remarried give themselves a better current outlook on life than those who did not remarry, or those who are either separated or widowed" (p. 3). Seventy-five percent of the women in the study said they'd made the right decision. Even so, more women than men (63% versus 44%) suffer greatly from stress. However, the rates of high stress and depression for both groups are about the same as singles ages 40–69.

According to the AARP study the age group of 60–70 indicated that they like doing things for themselves and having their own identity. However, what they dislike most is not having someone to do things with. Fifty-year-olds appear to have the most difficulty with divorce, indicating in the study that their divorce was more difficult than a major illness. However, the 50-year-olds liked not having to deal with another person.

Shapiro (2003) found that when compared to married fathers in stable relationships, fathers who divorced were more likely to experience a decline in weekly contact with their children. Divorced mothers were more likely than married mothers to report an increase in weekly contact with an adult child. Shapiro found, however, that divorce may slightly increase a mother's likelihood of little or no contact with an adult child.

When it came to sexuality, the AARP study found that after their divorce, people dated mainly to prove to themselves or to their ex-spouses that they were getting on with their lives. About a third (32%) remarried. A few of those in the study (6%) remarried the same person, or had sex with their spouse occasionally or often for several years after their divorce (4%). Over half reported sexual touching or hugging in varying degrees of frequency (daily to once or twice a month), while 38% had no sexual contact at all. Most women who had not remarried (69%) did not touch or hug at all sexually. An even larger number of women (77%) who had not remarried did not engage at all in sexual intercourse as opposed to half of the men who had not remarried.

KEEPING RELATIONSHIPS FROM FAILING

Even though there is a certain amount of cynicism about marriage and long-term relationships, there is good reason to want to save older adult relationships. For one thing, establishing new relationships as we age isn't easy. As we get older we also get a bit more set in our ways and inflexible. There are financial considerations that shouldn't be ignored in a time of financial difficulty in the country. Having and keeping a home that provides comfort and affordability is no small matter during a time when selling a home might result in a substantial loss. Most important, however, you should never give up on something that gave you pleasure and joy without trying to find ways of making the relationship better. There are a number of ways you can do that.

- There are couples weekends sponsored by many organizations, churches, and synagogues. These weekends are led by professionals, but the purpose is to help you communicate better and to reestablish the loving feelings you had earlier in the relationship. They are usually inexpensive and often lead to significant change. Before you attend a workshop you should get feedback from others who have attended in the past and from the leader to see if it will fit your needs.
- Setting aside times to talk during the day with the understanding that you will discuss the good and bad often helps resolve problems

before they become too difficult to resolve without professional help.

- A number of ministers and rabbis have professional training in couples work and might be helpful in resolving problems that are becoming difficult for either of you to handle. Professional mental health workers (social workers, psychologists, counselors, and psychiatrists) can be very helpful in saving relationships since they bring an objective point of view and are trained in problem solving. Some strong evidence, provided here, suggests that couples counseling can be very effective in maintaining relationships. In a review of the literature, Wills (2009) concluded that:
  1. At the end of couple's therapy, 75% of couples receiving therapy are better off than similar couples who did not receive therapy.
  2. 65% of couples report significant improvement.
  3. Most couples benefit from therapy, but both spouses will not necessarily experience the same outcomes or benefits.

Wills (2009) notes that "Couples today feel increasingly isolated and are expected to manage their lives and families without the community supports. With the aid of a qualified clinician, couples can bring peace, stability, and communication back into their relationship" (p. 1). She goes on to say that the purpose of couples therapy is to identify the presence of dissatisfaction and distress in the relationship, and to restore the relationship to a better and healthier level of functioning. Couples therapy can assist persons who are having complaints of intimacy, sexual, and communication difficulties.

PERSONAL STORY: COUPLES THERAPY HELPS A "HOPELESS" RELATIONSHIP

"Jane and I had been together for five years. The first year we lived apart but decided that since I was spending so much time at her place that we should live together for economic reasons and to be able to see each other more. I was 65 and Jane was 60. I thought Jane was very attractive and smart, although I also realized we came from very different backgrounds, had a big difference in education, and might not have a lot in common.

"Jane's condo was certainly nicer than mine. Since she worked during the day I had a lot of freedom. The city we were in was very congested and life there seemed very stressful to me. True, we had the benefits of many good restaurants and a lot of cultural activities, but I was never happy there.

"Once we started living together it was clear that many of the things I had concerns about became more obvious. Jane is a very detached and withdrawn person and often we would have nothing to say to one another unless I started the conversation. Jane also seemed stuck in the past and would often talk about her ex-husband even though they'd been divorced for 15 years. It made me wonder if she had ever gotten over the marriage, although she denied it. She could be very crass at times and swore a lot. It bothered me because, I suppose, I have traditional ideas about women, and men and women swearing still troubles me. Like me, Jane is a loner and doesn't have many friends. Most of our social contacts were with my friends and almost never with hers. The people she said I would like turned out to be pretty awful. Even she agreed they hadn't treated me well. These were friends she hadn't seen in many years and hadn't really kept up with. It didn't make me mad at her that they were so obnoxious toward me but it pretty much stopped us going out with any of her friends.

"Jane often spoke about us getting married but I strongly rejected the idea largely because I didn't want to be remarried and also because of my concerns with our relationship. I was often very unhappy in our relationship and we frequently had bad fights. Jane would go into a funk for days and would sleep for 14–16 hours and wouldn't talk to me until finally we'd have an emotional reconciliation and then, within days we'd go back to having problems. It was a pretty miserable couple of years with me gaining a lot of weight and not exercising the way I used to.

"We moved to a new community and bought a house together, a very bad idea, I thought, but I went along with it. I had no idea where I would live or who I would meet if we broke up, so I passively accepted the move. Both of us liked the new community and enjoyed fairly separate lives. About a year and a half into this new arrangement we could no longer avoid our problems and finally went for couples counseling. It was clear from the start that we had major problems. I would get angry at Jane and she would go into her shell for several days. We would always make up but the periods between my angry outbursts were getting shorter.

"I didn't really want to go for counseling and kept putting it off. I think of counseling as feminine, something for women and not men. To her credit Jane insisted that we go and with the sale of our house on the horizon and the possibility of us losing a lot of money, I finally agreed. We found the names of therapists online and after three or four calls found someone who seemed nice enough on the phone. Plus she had a doctorate in psychology which meant that she was certainly smart, which was important to me. I know that sounds pretty obnoxious but when I get help I want to know that the person I get help from (like doctors and dentists) are smart and nice. Competency matters.

"She let us talk and, much to my surprise, Jane had very strong feelings about my behavior, feelings she'd had a hard time discussing with me directly, but in the counselor's office she was brutally clear that I had temper problems and that I could be a real pain in the ass. It didn't make me happy to hear but it was clear that Jane was unhappy and that she'd reached the end of her willingness to put up with me. I thought she would put up with me no matter what but I was wrong. She brought up a number of idiosyncrasies I had that made her walk on eggshells a lot of the time. Like I hated any kind of noise or having her move stuff even though I dropped it indiscriminately wherever I felt like dropping it and didn't care how sloppy I was.

"The therapist was pretty calm about it all. She let us both talk and gave us a lot of space to confront each other with our grievances. When we finished she gave us things to work on and insisted we get together every night to resolve anything that happened during the day that bothered us to improve our ability to talk to each other. She also said we had to find more things to do together and to begin to get to know what we liked, and to share that in our evening chats. Up to this point we had almost felt like roommates, so the idea of doing things together was a little foreign to us, but we worked at it.

"To my surprise I discovered that Jane was a very well-read and intelligent woman who felt inferior to me because she wasn't as educated. I also discovered that she was better at a whole range of things than I was. It was pretty amazing to discover since up to that time I thought Jane was a very limited person—certainly, not up to my standards. It turned out that I was wrong, and as we continued in couple's therapy the meek withdrawn person I'd seen before therapy turned out to be a smart, assertive, and attractive woman. I had to admit that there weren't a lot of those around in my age range and that I was pretty fortunate to have her in my life.

"We saw the therapist eight times and now go once a month just to check in and make sure everything is OK. We've gotten pretty good at clearing the air before anything major happens, but when it does, and it does from time to time, we use the skills we learned in therapy to work them out.

"What did therapy do for me? It saved me from losing a very good mate. It saved me from having to sell our house and losing thousands of dollars. It saved me from starting all over again, something I feared and dreaded. It taught me a lot about how people really can change and that you shouldn't give up on someone you cared for in the past just because things aren't going well now. And it taught me something a lot of men don't know how to do and that's to ask for help when I can't work something out by myself. There's nothing wrong with that and the whole process wasn't at all feminizing. If anything it taught me to use the skills I have as a man to problem-solve and it made me better at using them.

"Jane and I are invited to a 4th of July party with a New Orleans theme. We're supposed to wear masks and bangles. I bumped into one of the guys who's invited who told me under no circumstance would he wear a stupid mask and bangles. You know what? The 'old me' would have said the same thing, but couples counseling helped me realize what a rigid, stick-in-the-mud, and unhappy person I was. I'm wearing the mask and bangles and I don't care how ridiculous they look. I'm going to have a good time and I don't care what he or anyone else thinks."—F. K.

SUMMARY

This chapter discusses divorce and breakups and what you can do to prevent them from happening. Divorce and breakups are traumatic at any age, but they're particularly painful for older adults who put great energy into relationships only to approach older age without a partner and perhaps with few prospects. A story giving the benefits of couples therapy is included to show that counseling and other ways of dealing with relationship problems can be very helpful, and that you shouldn't give up on relationships before seeking help.

REFERENCES

AARP (2004). "The Divorce Experience: A Study of Divorce at Midlife and Beyond." *Executive Summary*: 1–5.

Amato, P. R., and Booth, A. (1997). *A Generation at Risk*. Cambridge, MA: Harvard University Press.

Brinig, M. E., and Allen, D. A. (2000). "These Boots Are Made For Walking: Why Most Divorce Filers Are Women." *American Law and Economics Review* 2–1: 126–69.

Cherlin, A. (1992). *Marriage, Divorce, Remarriage*. Cambridge, MA: Harvard University Press.

Clarke, S. C. (1995). "Advance Report of Final Divorce Statistics, 1989 and 1990." *Monthly Vital Statistics Report* 43 (8). Hyattsville, MD: National Center for Health Statistics.

DeMaris, A., and Vaninadha Rao, K. (1992). "Premarital Cohabitation and Marital Instability in the United States: A Reassessment." *Journal of Marriage and the Family* 54: 178–90.

Fischer, H. "Why Him, Why Her?" Retrieved June 30, 2009 from: http://www.tellinitlikeitis.net/2009/01/why-him-why-her-helen-fisher-personality-test-understanding-your-personality-type.html.

Goldstein, J. R. (1999). "The Leveling of Divorce in the United States." *Demography* 36: 409–14.

Manfred, E. "Boomer Divorce." Retrieved February 8, 2009 from: http://heshistory.com/why-this-book/boomer-divorce/.

"Marital Transitions: Widowhood, Divorce and Remarriage." Retrieved June 25, 2009 from: http://family.jrank.org/pages/1039/Later-Life-Families-Marital-Transitions-Widowhood-Divorce-Remarriage.html.

Popenoe, D. "The Top Ten Myths of Divorce." Retrieved June 24, 2009 from: http://marriage.rutgers.edu/Publications/pubtoptenmyths.

Shapiro, A. (March 2003). "Later-Life Divorce and Parent–Adult Child Contact and Proximity: A Longitudinal Analysis." *Journal of Family Issues* 24 (2): 264–85.

Smock, P. J. (August 1993). "The Economic Costs of Marital Disruption for Young Women Over the Past Two Decades." *Demography* 30: 353–71.

——— (2000). "Cohabitation in the United States." *Annual Review of Sociology* 26: 1–20.

Tsing Loh, S. (June 22, 2009). "On Marriage: Let's Call the Whole Thing Off." *The Atlantic Online*. Retrieved June 23, 2009 from: http://www.msnbc.msn.com/id/31452178/ns/today_relationships//.

Uhlenberg, P., Cooney, T., and Boyd, R. (1990). "Divorce for Women After Midlife." *Journal of Gerontology: Social Science* 45: S3–S11.

Waite, L. J. (2004). Unpublished research cited in Waite, L. J., and Gallagher, M., *The Case for Marriage*. New York: Doubleday, 2000: 148.

Will, M. "The Effectiveness of Couples Counseling." Retrieved July 3, 2009 from: http://family-marriage-counseling.com/mentalhealth/couples-counseling.htm.

CHAPTER 6

Coping with Serious Illness and the Death of a Loved One

INTRODUCTION

Most older adults will experience the terminal illness and death of loved ones. Neither experience is pleasant, and while most of us grow emotionally from our loss, caring for a dying loved one and the grief following his or her death can often be an agonizing experience. In this chapter I'll discuss the impact of both experiences and suggest ways of coping with the experience.

TERMINAL ILLNESS

Christakis (2007) reports that physicians often fail to give terminally ill patients a prognosis and writes, "In one study of nearly 5,000 hospitalized adults who had roughly six months to live, only 15% were given clear prognoses. In a smaller study of 326 cancer patients in Chicago hospices, all of whom had about a month to live, only 37% of the doctors interviewed said they would share an accurate prognosis with their patients, and only if patients or their families pushed them to do so" (p. 1). The result, according to Christakis, is that doctors can make the end of life more difficult because "patients are given no chance to draft wills, see distant loved ones, make peace with estranged relatives or even discuss with their families their wishes about how to live the end of their lives. And they are denied the chance to make decisions about what kind of medical care they want to receive" (p. 1). Because doctors overestimate the time a patient has left to live by tripling it, patients are often encouraged to have needlessly painful and expensive medical procedures that complicate the end of life.

The CDC (2007) reports that, "More than one-third of U.S. deaths are preventable. Three behaviors—smoking, poor diet, and physical inactivity—were the root causes of almost 35% of U.S. deaths in 2000. These behaviors are risk factors that often underlie the development of the nation's leading chronic disease killers: heart disease, cancer, stroke, and diabetes" (p. 5).

Hardwig (2000) believes that people with terminal illnesses often suffer from an inability to find meaning in the last moments of their lives and are unable to deal with significant issues related to family and other loved ones. Often they feel "cast out" because they are no longer healthy or productive and feel as if they are a burden to others because they are unable to care for themselves, even in very basic ways. Hardwig suggests that people with terminal illnesses often feel isolated and angry about their lives and frequently feel abandoned by friends and family, and by God. Most of all, they feel betrayed by their own bodies and often have no way of dealing with the physical and emotional changes they are experiencing. Hardwig (2000) goes on to say that "Facing death brings to the surface questions about what life is all about. Long-buried assumptions and commitments are revealed. And many find that the beliefs and values they have lived by no longer seem valid or do not sustain them. These are the ingredients of a spiritual crisis, the stuff of spiritual suffering" (p. 29).

Hardwig found that the following problems facing people with terminal illness frequently create difficulty in finding meaning in the last moments of life: (1) The medical care system often takes important treatment decisions out of the hands of terminally ill patients and their loved ones; (2) use of painkilling drugs leaves dying patients unable to think clearly and distorts the days and weeks before death occurs; (3) no one listens to terminally ill patients or helps them resolve unfinished business; (4) in a death-denying society, families may not allow terminally ill patients to discuss issues that often help the terminally ill person find important life messages and also help the family with bereavement; (5) family members may not want to "let go" of a loved one and ignore the terminally ill patient's desire to end life naturally without intrusive life supports or treatments.

McClain and colleagues (2003) studied the spiritual well-being of terminally ill patients and found that low levels of spirituality correlated highly with "end-of-life despair, providing a unique contribution to the prediction of hopelessness, desire for hastened death, and suicidal [thoughts] even after controlling for the effect of depressive symptoms and other relevant variables" (p. 1606). The authors believe the most important single dynamic of spirituality is faith, since it provides hopefulness even during the end stages of terminal illness. The existence of hopefulness translates into cooperative relations with the medical staff, better resolution of interpersonal and family problems, and a desire to live longer.

In summarizing successful coping strategies used by seriously and/or terminally ill patients, Livneh (2000) suggests the following strategies:

1. **Problem-focused/-solving Coping and Information Seeking.** These strategies refer to resolution of the stress and anxiety of illness through information-gathering, focused planning, and direct action-taking. These approaches have had positive effects on global mental health (Chen et al. 1996), have lead to decreased levels of depression and anxiety (Mishel and Sorenson 1993), and have increased vigor (Mishel and Sorenson).

2. **Fighting Spirit and Confrontation.** These strategies are described as accepting a serious and perhaps life-threatening diagnosis while optimistically challenging, tackling, confronting, and recovering from the illness. A fighting spirit and confrontation have been linked to longer survival among people diagnosed with cancer (Greer 1991), to decreased anxiety and depression (Burgess, Morris, and Pettingale 1988), and to decreased emotional or psychological distress (Classen, Koopman, Angell, and Spiegel 1996).

3. **Focusing on Positives.** This group of coping strategies has been associated with psychological well-being (Ell, Mantell, Hamovitch, and Nishimoto 1989), lower emotional distress (Carver et al. 1993), and increased vigor (Schnoll et al. 1995).

4. **Self-restraint.** This strategy refers to personal control to cope with the stresses of a serious or terminal disease and is a predictor of lower emotional distress (Morris 1986) but may also lead to a reduction of quality of life among survivors of such illnesses as cancer (Wagner, Armstrong, and Laughlin 1995).

5. **Seeking Social Support.** Seeking support and assistance from others has been linked to decreased emotional/psychological distress (Stanton and Snider 1993), better adaptation to life (Heim et al. 1997), and a greater perceptions of well-being (Filipp et al. 1990).

6. **Expressing Feelings, or Venting.** While the evidence is mixed, two studies show decreased depression (Chen et al. 1996) and

better emotional control (Classen et al. 1996) when venting (telling others openly how you feel or think about issues) of feelings takes place. The negative aspect of this coping strategy is that angry patients sometimes allienate loved ones and the professional staff, which may lead to increased feelings of depression and loss of social supports in patients.

7. **Using Humor:** Carver and colleagues (1993) found that the use of humor resulted in decreased emotional distress among people with cancer.

8. **Finding Increased Life Meaning:** Many writers discuss the potential for increased meaning of life as a result of serious or terminal illnesses. McClain, Rosenfeld, and Breitbart (2003) found that high levels of spirituality in dying patients lead to hopefulness that resulted in a more cooperative relationship with the treatment team, improved resolution of long-standing emotional problems, and the desire to live longer. Finn (1999) believes that spirituality leads to "an unfolding consciousness about the meaning of human existence. Life crises influence this unfolding by stimulating questions about the meaning of existence" (p. 487). Balk (1999) suggests that three issues must be present for a life crisis to result in spiritual changes: "The situation must create a psychological imbalance or disequilibrium that resists readily being stabilized; there must be time for reflection; and the person's life must forever afterwards be colored by the crisis" (p. 485). Kübler-Ross (1969, 1997) believes that terminal illness often leads to life-changing growth and new and more complex behaviors that focus on meaning-of-life issues.

BEREAVEMENT

Death of friends and loved ones is a reality of aging, but it is also one that many of us have difficulty coping with. This section discusses bereavement and the many ways of coping with loss.

Balk (1999) indicates that bereavement, the loss of a significant person in one's life, can result in physical and emotional problems, the most significant of which may include:

Intense and long-lasting reactions such as fear, anger, and sorrow. Bereavement affects cognitive functioning (e.g., memory distortions, attention deficits, and ongoing vigilance for danger) and behavior (e.g., sleep disturbances, excessive drinking, increased

cigarette smoking, and reckless risk taking). It impacts social relationships as outsiders to the grief become noticeably uncomfortable
when around the bereaved. And bereavement affects spirituality by
challenging the griever's very assumptions about the meaning of
human existence. (Balk 1999, p. 486)

Jacobs and Prigerson (2000) suggest that while symptoms of
bereavement may include all of those noted by Balk, bereavement
sometimes develops into a very long-term problem, which the researchers describe as "complicated or prolonged grief" lasting more than a
year. The symptoms associated with complicated grief include highly
intrusive thoughts about the deceased, numbness, disbelief, feeling
dazed, and a loss of a sense of security. Complicated bereavement lasts
longer and is more intense than the normal symptoms of depression
following the loss of a loved one.

Balk (1999) believes that bereavement is a catalyst for spiritual
change because it triggers a life-threatening crisis that, in turn, threat-
ens "well-being, challenges established coping repertoire, and over
time, produces harmful and/or beneficial outcomes" (p. 486).

The loss of a spouse is among the most stressful life events most of us
will ever experience. Although widowhood is often expected by older
women because they tend to live longer than men, the duration and
severity of a spouse's terminal illness shapes the way most older adults
experience loss and may negatively affect marital satisfaction, which
can lead to guilt and prolonged bereavement following the death of a
spouse. More men remarry after the loss of a spouse than women. This
may be due to the greater number of potential marriage partners. However, the generally low rates of remarriage among older men and women
following the loss of a spouse may also be due to fears of social disap-
proval, financial concerns, and the opposition of other family members.
Studies of attitudes toward remarriage indicate that older women are
often reluctant to remarry because they don't want to give up their freedom, are not interested in establishing a new sexual relationship, don't
want to go through the loss of another husband, fear the reactions of
their children, feel that it would be disloyal to their deceased husband,
and don't want to take on additional domestic responsibilities.

HELP IN REDUCING THE SYMPTOMS OF GRIEF

Piper and colleagues (2002) studied the relationship between the
expression of positive affect (smiles, nods in agreement, sympathetic

looks) in group therapy and favorable treatment outcomes for compli-cated (long-lasting) grief. The authors found a strong positive correla-tion between these two variables in a number of therapy groups studied. The authors believe that positive affect conveys optimism in the person and has a positive effect on others in the group. The authors also found positive affect to correlate well with a cooperative attitude and a desire to do the work necessary to resolve the complicated and traumatic grief they were experiencing. This was true regardless of the type of counseling that was offered. Affect, rather than the approach, was the overriding factor in successful resolution of prolonged grief.

Kendall (1994) found cognitive-behavioral therapy (a type of therapy that uses rational thinking and logic) to be effective with chil-dren suffering from separation anxiety after the death of a loved one. The authors report that treated children had reduced fears, less anxi-ety, better social skills, and lower scores on depression inventories. These gains continued in follow-up a year after the end of treatment. The authors are uncertain if this same finding would be applicable to adults suffering from prolonged grief.

Jacobs and Prigerson (2000) report that self-help groups have been effective, to some extent, by "offering the inculcation of hope, the development of understanding, social supports, a source of normaliza-tion or universalization, and a setting to learn and practice new coping skills" (p. 487). Raphael (1977) studied a three-month type of therapy that used insight and an examination of the past for high-risk, acutely traumatized widows during the first stages of grief. The author defined high risk as the lack of support by a social network, the sud-denness or unexpected nature of the death, high levels of anger and guilt, ambivalent feelings about the marital relationship, and the pres-ence of other life crises related to or predating the death of a spouse. The predating life crises were often financial or work-related or involved children, substance abuse in the spouse of widow/widower, or marital infidelity. When compared to the group not getting help, the treatment group had better general health, was less anxious and depressed, and had fewer health symptoms.

CASE STUDY: HELP FOR PROLONGED GRIEF

Thanks to Elsevier, Inc. for permission to use the following case study, which first appeared in a book on aging for professionals in the human service field (Glicken 2009, pp. 377–79).

Ellen Steward is a 63-year-old mother of three adult children whose husband passed away suddenly following a major heart attack. Ellen's husband was a health fanatic who worked out daily, often in preference to spending time with her. Jonathan, Ellen's 67-year-old husband, thought he was experiencing chest pains in the middle of the night but, as is the case with some heart victims in extreme denial, he went to the gym at 4:00 a.m. and began working out until he passed out and was pronounced dead at the scene. Ellen was left with a large number of debts, no insurance, and few benefits beyond social security.

Jonathan passed away over a year ago but Ellen had traumatic grief as noted by severe depression, high levels of anxiety, very angry and intrusive thoughts about Jonathan and the financial condition he left her in, and obsessive thoughts about what she wished she'd said to him before he died—uncomplimentary and angry remarks that conveyed her depth of despair over her current situation. Her physician referred Ellen to a counselor when she continued to complain of prolonged grief more than a year after Jonathan's death.

Ellen's therapist met with her and they immediately began a discussion of what was keeping Ellen from resolving her feelings of grief. Ellen was stymied, so the therapist suggested that she make a list of everything that came to mind, and that she also do some reading about the usual causes of prolonged grief and the best evidence of how to treat it so that they might continue the discussion at the next session. Ellen was initially angry that she was asked to do work that the therapist should be doing for her and complained to her referring physician, who encouraged her to give it a little more time. She halfheartedly did what the therapist had asked of her and returned only slightly prepared for further discussions at the next meeting.

When asked why she wasn't better prepared, Ellen became angry and confrontational. "You haven't even said you're sorry about my predicament," she said, and angrily confronted the therapist for doing what her husband always did: leaving decisions up to her. The therapist said she appreciated the feedback and *did* feel badly about Ellen's predicament. Still, she wondered why Ellen was unprepared and explained that only by working together could they resolve Ellen's painful and extended grief. Ellen promised to do more for the next session and, with the help of her precocious 10-year-old granddaughter, she was able to find Internet articles that seemed to very clearly explain why her grief wasn't going away and what she might do about it.

The next session with the therapist was very businesslike and purposeful. Ellen was excited about what she'd read and described it to her therapist. Together they planned the following strategy to treat Ellen's symptoms of prolonged grief:

(1) Ellen needed to discuss all the reasons for her anger at Jonathan. The therapist urged her to write them down and to bring the list with her the next session. Before she could resolve her anger with Jonathan, she had to be clear about *all* the reasons for her anger, even if they seemed illogical or suggested that Ellen's anger was unfounded. (2) If there was anything she could directly do about her anger, she would do it. Examples included trying to develop a strategy to help with finances, including a return to work. (3) She would join a self-help group for prolonged grief begun by a remarkable woman who had also gone through prolonged grief after the death of her 15-year-old son in a car crash. (4) Ellen would be seen by a psychiatrist to evaluate the use of anti-depressive medications and to supervise the medical treatment of her depression. (5) She would start a daily regimen of exercise and diet supervised by a nutritionist provided through her health care plan. (6) Her spiritual and religious ties had been broken after Jonathan's death. She missed both and planned to reestablish them. (7) She had distanced herself from Jonathan's family. While she had been close to them when Jonathan was alive, she felt irrationally angry and blamed them for Jonathan's obsessive worry about his physical condition. Jonathan's father had begun having heart attacks in his mid-forties. Ellen felt they had done too little to moderate Jonathan's anxiety about his health and subtly encouraged his overindulgence in exercise. Ellen decided that it was important for her to reestablish her contact with the family because she and her children missed them. (8) She would continue on in treatment for at least 12 sessions.

Ellen's prolonged grief began to moderate itself after two months of treatment. By the third month she was back to her old self, although she still attended the self-help group and saw the therapist once a month to monitor her depression. She no longer takes anti-depressive medications, has maintained her exercise regimen and diet, and sees her in-laws regularly. She still has difficulty reestablishing her religious ties and continues to blame God for taking her husband. "Maybe I'll never feel the same way," she said, "but you never know. I keep hoping and, of course, I go to synagogue on the High Holy Days, but most of it just makes me mad and I think that maybe I'm a spiritual person but not a religious one."

THE COUNSELOR'S COMMENTS

In commenting on Ellen's grief the therapist said:

I don't know that I would call her depression prolonged. It seems to me that people experience grief in their own unique way and Ellen's quick recovery, once she was in therapy, is a good example of how people respond to death and how therapy can be a helping process. Giving people assignments to help in their own recovery is energizing, and encouraging their own involvement in treatment can be very empowering. Ellen needed a little push and then she was better. She'll have moments of sorrow and despair. When you love someone and they pass on before their time, you expect that to happen. But on every measure of life functioning, Ellen is doing a great deal better. From the paucity of good sound evidence of best evidence to prolonged treat grief, one can't help but think that even at a professional level, we are still a death-denying society. One last thought. Grief and depression are two separate issues. Yes, people in grief feel depressed but you have to treat the grief as a separate issue. Many people find it hard to talk about death but you can't really help people cope with the death of a loved one without talking about the impact it's had. And you have to talk to people about their own notions of death because that's what drives their grief. In Ellen's case, she had begun losing her religious faith even before her husband died. The reasons are complex but she had a very confused relationship with her faith and yet was obligated by family pressure to give her husband a religious funeral. It was very confusing to her. She says she hasn't been able to reconnect with her religious beliefs, and while I've encouraged that she try, it doesn't feel right to her and she's begun attending a group that discusses spirituality. It suits her needs now but at some point in time it may be important for her to have further discussions about her faith and why it's left her.

PERSONAL STORY: RECONNECTING WITH AN ABSENT TERMINALLY ILL PARENT

The author wishes to thank Elsevier Publications for permission to use this story, which first appeared in the author's book on aging (Glicken 2009, pp. 361–62).

"My husband's parents divorced when Jack was 17; his father was an alcoholic, and Jack saw little of his father after the divorce. When Jack was in his thirties, he reconnected briefly with his father, but saw him intermittently. Ten years later, Jack's father contacted him once more. He was dying and wanted to see his son. Jack and his sister Letty drove 75 miles to visit their father. Letty had been in touch with her father, but as his health began to fail, he was often talking about seeing Jack again. Letty knew that Jack was reluctant to talk to his father, having many old feelings which were painful. 'Better to let sleeping dogs lie,' was his usual saying. It was a strangely calm meeting. Their father, Joe, had been recently diagnosed with pancreatic cancer, and was given a terminal diagnosis of an expected life of only 30 days remaining. Joe had opted to have hospice care and remain at the nursing home, where he had lived for the past three months.

"Jack and Letty were quickly able to set aside old resentments, recognizing that their father did not have long to live. Joe had obviously been thinking a lot about this reunion. 'I know I haven't been much of a father to either of you,' he told Jack, 'but I don't have much time left. I figured we might spend some of it on the important things.'

"They spent some time talking to their father before he became quite tired, and needed to rest. Letty and Jack spoke to the nurse at the nursing home, who filled them in on Joe's care. They made an appointment to meet with the hospice social worker the next day.

"Over the course of the next several weeks, Jack and Letty spent hours with their father. The nursing home had a courtyard, and so they pushed their father's wheelchair outside in the afternoons so he could enjoy the flowers and the sunshine. They talked over past times, good and bad, and had the opportunity to make amends for a number of issues from the past.

"Jack said, 'good, bad, or ugly, you're my father, and I'm grateful for this last chance to set some things right.' Joe said he wasn't in much pain, and his hospice nurse took good care of him. The social worker helped them talk about funeral plans, what to expect, and opened the door for many conversations they had never expected to have.

"On the day Joe died, Letty and Jack had just come back from lunch. Joe was only briefly awake that day, and opened his eyes to say, 'It isn't so bad now. Thank you.' Later, Jack and Letty recalled that moment many times and felt, for them, and in their situation, it summed up a lifetime. Jack said, 'That was the best gift my father could have given us. Hospice helped us have that time with our father. He wasn't much of a father when he was alive, but we felt we owed each other something, nevertheless.' And there was peace in that."—S. Y. B.

SUMMARY

This chapter on terminal illness and the death of loved ones discusses the ways in which one can cope with both difficult and often emotionally troubling events in the lives of older adults. Older adults have more than their share of friends, family members, and spouses who pass on. The death of loved ones can sometimes move a person into prolonged grief, a type of bereavement that is persistent and may last a long time. A case study shows how counseling can be helpful in dealing with the prolonged grief of an older woman.

REFERENCES

Balk, D. E. (1999). "Bereavement and Spiritual Change." *Death Studies* 23 (6): 485–93.

Casarett, D., Van Ness, P. H., O'Leary, J. R., and Fried, T. R. (2006). "Are Patient Preferences for Life-Sustaining Treatment Really a Barrier to Hospice Enrollment for Older Adults with Serious Illness?" *Journal of the American Geriatrics Society* 54 (3): 472–78.

Duggleby, W. (August 2005). "Transitions and Shifting Goals of Care for Palliative Patients and Their Families." *Clinical Journal of Oncology Nursing* 9 (4): 425–28.

Gazelle, G. (July 26, 2007). "Understanding Hospice—An Underutilized Option for Life's Final Chapter." *New England Journal of Medicine* 357 (4): 321–24.

Jacobs, S., and Prigerson, H. (2000). "Psychotherapy of Traumatic Grief: A Review of Evidence for Psychotherapeutic Treatments."*Death Studies* 2 (6): 479–96.

Kane, R. L., Wales, J., Bernstein, L., Leibowitz, A., and Kaplan, S. A. (1984). "Randomized Controlled Trial of Hospice Care." *Lancet* 824 (8408): 890–92.

Kendall, P. C. (1994). "Treating Anxiety Disorders in Children: Results of a Randomized Clinical Trial." *Journal of Consulting and Clinical Psychology* 62: 100–110.

Medicare (2004). *Medicare Benefit Policy Manual.* Retrieved December 1, 2007 from: http://www.cms.hhs.gov/manuals/Downloads/bp102c09.pdf.

Miller, S. C., Intrator, O., Gonzalo, P., Roy, J., Barber, J., and Mor, V. (2004). "Government Expenditures at the End of Life for Short- and Long-Stay

Nursing Home Residents: Differences by Hospice Enrollment Status." *Journal of the American Geriatrics Society* 52 (8): 1284–92.

Miller, S. C., Mor, V., and Teno, J. (2003). "Hospice Enrollment and Pain Assessment and Management in Nursing Homes." *Journalof Pain Symptom Management* 26: 791–99.

National Hospice and Palliative Care Organization (2007). *NHPCO Facts and Figures: Hospice Care in America*, November 2007 Edition. http://www .nhpco.org/files/public/Statistics_Research/NHPCO_facts-and-figures _Nov2007.pdf.

Piper, W. E., Ogrodniczuk, J. S., Joyce, A. S., and McCallum, M. R. (2002). "Relationships among Affect, Work, and Outcome in Group Therapy for Patients with Complicated Grief." *American Journal of Psychotherapy* 56 (6): 347–62.

Rand Corporation (February 16, 2004). "Rand Study Finds Choosing Hospice Care Raises Medicare Costs for the Last Year of Life." http://www .rand.org/news/press.04/02.16.html.

Raphael, B. (1977). "Preventive Intervention with the Recently Bereaved." *Archives of General Psychiatry* 34: 1450–54.

Rhodes, R. L. (September 2006). "Racial Disparities in Hospice: Moving from Analysis to Intervention." *Virtual Mentor* 6 (9): 612–16.

Stroebe, M. S. (2001). "Bereavement Research and Theory: Retrospective and Prospective." *American Behavioral Scientist* 44 (5): 854–65.

Teno, J. M., Clarridge, B. R., Casey, V., et al. (2004). "Family Perspectives on End-of-Life Care at the Last Place of Care." *Journal of the American Medical Association* 291: 88–93.

U.S. Department of Health and Human Services (2005). *Medicare Hospice Benefits*. Retrieved December 1, 2007 from: http://www.medicare.gov/ publications/pubs/pdf/02154.pdf.

Welch, L. C., Teno, J. M., and Mor, V. (2006). "End-of-Life Care in Black and White: Race Matters for Medical Care of Dying Patients and Their Families." *Journal of the American Geriatric Society* 53: 1145–53.

Winter, L., Parker, B., and Schneider, M. (2007). "Imagining the Alternatives to Life Prolonging Treatments: Elders' Beliefs about the Dying Experience." *Death Studies* 31 (7): 619–31.

Zimmermann, C. (2004). "Denial of Impending Death: A Discourse Analysis of the Palliative Care Literature." *Social Science & Medicine* 59 (8): 1769–80.

CHAPTER 7

Single and Sometimes Lonely: Good Friends and Lovers Can Help

INTRODUCTION

It's not unusual to worry about being single as you age. There are a number of commonly held beliefs that single people are lonelier than married people, have more illnesses at an earlier point in their retirement, are unhappier than their married counterparts, and enjoy life less. A brief look at some of the literature on retired singles confirms these popular beliefs. For example, Gamm (2008) writes about the fear of emotional loneliness and "the lack of someone to share dinner with in the evenings, someone to share time with on the weekend, and someone to look after you when you are not well" (p. 1). Gamm also says that:

> Becoming single can simplify and complicate the issues of retirement. First, you now only have yourself to think about—no in-laws to worry about, no worrying about your partner's health. You basically can do what you want to do! Conversely, you now don't have a partner to share things with or for emotional support. It means being deprived of the comfort of a partner and possibly may mean isolation and loneliness.

While these concerns may be true for some retired singles, and loneliness is certainly everything it's cracked up to be, there are a number of single older men and women who live well, are happy and healthy, and are anything but lonely. This chapter is about ways to be socially involved with and without a partner. Many of us do it without a partner and thrive.

LONELINESS AMONG OLDER SINGLES

Hawkley and Cacioppo (2007) report that loneliness causes more rapid declines in health than in older adults who are not lonely. This finding supports a popular belief that loneliness is a destructive force in our lives and that older adults who are lonely (and without a partner) are particularly likely to suffer health problems because of the association between loneliness and depression. However, they also report that there are few well-done pieces of research to support this contention and very few studies showing higher rates of loneliness for single older adults. Married couples can also experience loneliness as a result of shifts in their relationship and empty nest syndrome. Interestingly, the researchers write that having friends and other social contacts can reduce and even eliminate loneliness in the absence of a partner.

There are a number of reasons we feel lonely. For some of us, loneliness is a lifelong condition having a great deal to do with our early life experiences. Children who fail to bond with troubled parents often experience lifelong loneliness. This type of loneliness needs the assistance of a very good mental health professional, since people with lifelong feelings of loneliness often experience loneliness even when they are in intimate relationships, with friends, or in social situations. Others feel lonely in later life as a result of a divorce, the end of a long-term relationship, or the death of a spouse. And yet others begin to experience loneliness as the result of the death of parents, friends, or declining health. All of these situations should be thought of as serious indicators of the need for professional help. Merely increasing your social contacts may work for many people, but when it doesn't, you need to put your pride aside and seek professional help.

There are other reasons for feeling lonely, many having to do with being discounted as we age. Our society is a youth-oriented one that assumes older adults have less to contribute as we age. This form of ageism often drives perfectly capable older adults from productive and enjoyable jobs and makes them believe that their productive lives are over once they reach retirement age. Rokach and Neto (2005) found a significant difference in a Canadian population in which culture was factored into the measure of loneliness. Older adults from traditional cultures in which age is considered a sign of wisdom were far less likely to feel lonely than those from the normative culture in North America. Many social scientists believe that an important reason older adults may experience more loneliness is that they've been marginalized by a culture that defines them as nonproductive and non-contributing. Older single adults who have been downsized or forced from jobs because of age are more likely to experience loneliness in retirement because a primary place to meet people and form friendships has been taken from them.

One of the mistakes that older single men and women make is to load up their lives with activities and people with whom they have superficial relationships. Granted, it's better to be socially active than not, but when people are really in need because of a crisis, superficial friendships are almost always disappointing. One older single woman told me that when she injured her leg in a car accident and was home-bound for many months, she had few visitors or phone calls from the many people she thought were good friends. Obviously they weren't. A retired single man told me that in the midst of a severe episode of rapid heartbeat he could not stop, he called a female friend with whom he thought he had a strong relationship who told him to call an ambulance because she didn't want to spend time at the hospital waiting for him. There is a quantum difference between a friend you can count on and an acquaintance you can't.

OLDER SINGLES AND LOVE

Almost half of the people 65 and older in the United States are single. According to Perman (2006), many older adults simply date without necessarily wanting to remarry. Living Apart Together (LAT) is a type of relationship in which partners define themselves as a couple, see each other often, but maintain separate residences. Creating this form of relationship may stem from job demands, responsibilities to family members, etc., but for others it offers sufficient intimacy and also provides time to see friends, have secure finances, and be involved in activities they enjoy, but which their partners may not. For women, maintaining their own homes may constitute financial security and avoids commingling finances and the problems that may arise from misunderstandings about money, unequal responsibilities, or broken relationships.

Some states have wisely given older adults the opportunity to have domestic partnerships in which one of the partners might receive the medical benefits of the other. Often people who enter into domestic partnerships have a type of prenuptial agreement that serves to protect them financially should the relationship end. Domestic partnerships have many of the legal constraints of marriage but fewer benefits. Income tax, for example, must be paid as a single taxpayer and joint returns are disallowed under federal and state guidelines.

INTERNET DATING

Should you use an Internet dating service to meet eligible men and women? There are certainly advantages in that you can control whom you meet. However, people often lie about their age or show pictures of themselves that are 10 or even 20 years younger (you shouldn't do this because it offends people when they meet). Smart but somewhat wacky people can seem healthy online but really aren't in person. It's best to have some phone conversations before meeting and then meet somewhere public where the issue of who pays the bill isn't a problem (a coffee house, for example). The process can be challenging because not everyone you meet is as nice as they appear online. Just remember that it takes kissing a lot of frogs before you kiss the czar or czarina of your heart. It also takes time and patience, but many people find that Internet dating often works amazingly well.

Dating services that have you videotape an interview and then have pictures and bios of men and women you might be interested in often charge $1,500–3,000 a year. Perhaps there are good ones, but I've heard numerous complaints about the lack of professionalism among the staff and the lack of interesting people to meet. Many people I talk to say the dating service staff members are mainly interesting in selling the dating service and seldom help members find suitable people to contact. Check dating services out carefully. It might be better just to use Internet dating services such as Match.com, E-Harmony, Jdate, and others that are much cheaper and include members who live in areas you initially might find undesirable because of distance, but who are worth getting to know. Older retired people often have the time to travel or develop long distance relationships, and it's a shame to pass up a good person because of distance.

Malta (2009) found that older adults who used the Internet to meet people were able to develop a relationship much more quickly than those who met face to face. While both groups develop sexual intimacy fairly soon after meeting, the face to face relationships lasted longer. The author writes that

Online relationships appear to happen more quickly than face to face romances (those developed at work or in other social contacts).

This, in itself, may also have had an impact on the longevity of the relationships. Perhaps relationships which take longer to develop through face-to-face contact have a more solid foundation going forward—or it may be that those involved feel they have invested more time and energy in the relationship and are not prepared to give them up quite as readily as Online ones. However, whether this makes relationships that begin face to face more "successful" in the long-term is open to conjecture. (p. 14)

CRUISES AND TRIPS TAKEN ALONE

Cruises are great ways to meet people. Many cruise lines offer single supplements that are about 75 percent more expensive than sharing a cabin. Given how inexpensive cruises are these days you can still do an affordable cruise and have the privacy of your own cabin. Most cruise lines allow as many as 3–4 people in a cabin. If money is an issue, having friends join you on a cruise is a very inexpensive way to go. Many cruise lines charge just $100 for a third person sharing a cabin. When the cruise price is divided by three people, it becomes fairly inexpensive. And remember, a cruise includes the cost of meals. The only extras that you need to pay for are drinks (soft and hard), tips, and land excursions. Many organizations have singles cruises whose sole purpose is to provide singles with a way to meet other singles. You may not find your mate this way but you can often meet some very nice people who may become friends and future travel partners.

There are a number of organizations online that will help you find people to share trips with. One such organization is Travel Chums (http://www.travelchums.com/), which maintains a Web site to help you find interesting trips with others. A recent posting found a hiking trip through Israel and Jordan and many postings to share trips to Argentina and Australia. These trips allow you to do some very interesting and adventurous trips with others who share similar desires to see specific places.

Some organizations waive the single supplement. A recent look at the Web site maintained by Overseas Adventure Travel (http://www.oattravel.com/gcc/general/) found inexpensive trips with some trips waiving the single supplements and offering singles a private room. A single friend just went to China for three weeks using Overseas Adventure Travel and told me the cost of the trip included airfare, lodging, and food. She said she was never lonely. The group she went with was small (about 20 people she didn't know), there were other singles, and people were very friendly. She said a few people were loners (she wasn't), and in her opinion, if you want to have a great time, a small guided trip like the one she went on is a great way to have a travel adventure and meet some very nice people at the same time.

PERSONAL STORY: SINGLE TO MARRIED?

The following e-mail was written by an older woman living with her domestic partner, a man in his late sixties. They bought a house together but never married. In the following e-mail she tells him about how not being married makes her feel.

"I have been feeling lately that the important people in my life have been letting me down. I like to think of myself as being independent—someone who doesn't ask much of those around her, and yet I'm feeling, well, sort of taken for granted? Superfluous? Incidental? I feel in a way that those for whom I should be important are setting me aside, putting me on the periphery of their lives, making me feel marginal.

"Leah [her daughter] keeps telling me how she leads such a busy life, and I feel that she thinks I'm not important enough for her to make the effort. Just recently, I called her to find out about her Hawaiian vacation and she told me she was so busy, and she'd call me in the next few days to tell me all about it. Nothing. She then called me on Mother's Day and proceeded to tell me she'd bought me a Mother's Day card, but hadn't gotten around to mailing it. We then discussed her and Jake [her son-in-law] and Zoe [her granddaughter] coming out for a visit, but that she'd have to check Jake's schedule, and she'd call me later that day or the next. Nothing.

"When I was a child my mother had a tendency to make me feel that I just wasn't an important part of her life—that in a way I didn't merit or deserve her attention. Now I'm feeling that my daughter feels the same way. My mother's messages are being reinforced. I am superfluous, incidental, and I only inhabit the margins of her life.

"And then there's you, Wade. You are so much an important part of my life I can't begin to express it. I don't think I ask much of the people in my life, and yet I'm feeling empty and taken for granted by my daughter and, most distressingly, you. From time to time I fall into a depression and a deep sense of sadness that my importance to you has limits. That you'll only go so far and no further in committing to me.

That the feelings my mother instilled in me are being reinforced again—I'm not important enough—I'm not worthy."—K. R.

SUMMARY

This chapter discusses single life. For many older singles, life is good and intimacy needs are often met. For some singles, however, life can be lonely, particularly for those who have moved to new communities assuming that they will easily meet other singles. The process of meeting good friends and the special people who will meet our personal needs as friends and lovers can take time. The chapter discusses ways of meeting people and potential mates using Internet dating and singles events and ends with a personal story by an older single woman who wants to marry and her feeling that the man's unwillingness is an indication that he doesn't trust or love her.

GREAT PLACES TO MEET PEOPLE

1. Osher Lifelong Learning Programs for older adults, found in almost all universities, junior, and community colleges: Go to your local university and/or community college to check out programs.
2. Tennis clubs in the United States: http://www.tennismates.com/clubs.asp.
3. American Association of University Women: http://www.aauw.org/.
4. Chamber of Commerce: For listing of local programs go to: http://www.chamberofcommerce.com/public/index.cfm?
5. League of Women Voters: http://www.lwv.org/AM/Template.cfm?Section=Home.
6. Readers Circle: A listing of local book clubs: http://www.readers circle.org/.
7. Peak to Peak: A comprehensive list of American hiking clubs: http://www.peaktopeak.net/clubs.html.
8. Singles organizations for single people: A state by state list of singles organizations: http://www.singlesorganizations.com/.
9. A great Web site for those interested in higher education: Association of Retired Organizations in Higher Education (AROHE): http://www.arohe.org/.

10. Investopedia: An excellent Web site about investment clubs sponsored by Forbes magazine that includes local investment clubs around the country: http://www.investopedia.com/articles/01/062001.asp.

11. For those of you who want advice on how to look your best for dating, a very good website to get professional help from someone with an advanced degree in social work is: http://www.linkedin.com/in/tamaredelsteinnaiditch.

REFERENCES

Gamm, J. "The Social Stigma of the Retired Single Female." Retrieved July 17, 2009 from: http://ezinearticles.com/?The-Social-Stigma-of-the-Retired-Single-Female&id=727723.

Hawkley, L. C., and Cacioppo, J. T. (2007). "Aging and Loneliness—Downhill Quickly: Current Directions in the Psychological Sciences." *Association for Psychological Sciences* 16 (4): 187.

Malta, S. (2007). "Intimacy and Older Adults: A Comparison between Online and Offline Romantic Relationships." *Australian Journal of Emerging Technologies and Society* 5 (2): 84–102.

Perman, D. (February 2, 2006). "The Changing Face of Romance in 2006: Are Valentines Just for the Young?" *Intimacy and Aging: Tips for Sexual Health and Happiness. UBC Reports* 52 (2).

Rokach, A., and Neto, R. (2005). "Age, Culture and the Antecedents of Loneliness." *Social Behavior and Personality* 33 (5): 477–94.

Stein, R. (August 23, 2007). "Elderly Staying Sexually Active." *Washington Post.* http://www.washingtonpost.com/wp-dyn/content/article/2007/08/22/AR2007082202000_pf.html.

Zernike, K. (November 18, 2007). "Still Many-Splendored: Love in the Time of Dementia." *New York Times.* http://www.nytimes.com/2007/11/18/weekinreview/18.

CHAPTER 8

Friends or Just Acquaintances

INTRODUCTION

We all know that having friends in our lives, good friends, is a blessing as we age. Friends are those trusting, loyal people who are there for us in a crisis and remain loyal even when there are conflicts between us. Acquaintances are people in our lives but they don't have the same level of loyalty. They come and go and we usually don't think of them as close friends. Unfortunately, we often confuse acquaintances with friends and it sometimes leads to unhappiness.

When the elements of good friendships were evaluated by age, Schnittker (2007) found that older adults expect "agreeableness" in their friends, or the ability to get along. Not surprisingly, the researcher also found that we base our concept of friendships on the early messages given to us by parents about our friends. Favorable feedback about friends at an early age can have a lasting impact on whom we consider to be friendship material.

Paul (2004) says new research suggests that friendships profoundly impact our physical and emotional health by boosting our immune system, protecting us from anxiety and depression, and improving our memory as well as our ability to sleep well. She goes on to say that while men need friendships, they often tend to turn to their wives for many of the things friends do, largely because women tend to be more soothing and comforting in relationships. She points out that one study found that when women and men were placed in stressful situations, people who were placed with women had lower stress levels than people who were placed with men. She believes the reason this happened is because women are better listeners, and are much less likely than men to try to fix things by giving unwanted advice. Whether this is true depends on your personal experiences but I've found women to be better listeners than men and more interested in concerns about intimate issues.

Chen (2009) notes that, "Many studies have shown the benefits of friendship on positive social, emotional, and physical well-being. Having a strong circle of friends can be a good source for aging hearts and help the body's autoimmune system resist disease. People who have one or more good friends have better health than those who have only casual friends or no friends" (p. 1). Chen also says that many older people live alone and lack even one good friend. She notes that in the United States, one out of every three women and one of every seven men aged 65 or older lives alone. She also finds that men have a harder time dealing with their widowhood than women. About two-thirds of older men reported that they did not have a close friend, while 16 percent of widows reported having no friends.

Regarding differences between men and women and the way they define friendships, Felmlee and Muraco (2009) found that women in later-life stages placed more emphasis on intimacy in their friendships than men did and also had higher expectations of friends. The researchers found that women were "more disapproving of violations of friendship rules, such as betraying a confidence, paying a surprise visit, and failing to stand up for a friend in public" (p. 317). However, men and women share important notions of friendship that are based on trust, commitment, and respect. These general notions of friendship remain throughout the life span and are as true for younger people as they are for older adults.

Parents discuss issues of friendship with children and help us define the attributes of friendships. One single older adult I know said that his mother's favorite expression was "better a good friend nearby than a family member far away." What she meant was that we often rely on friends more than family. For my friend's mother, friendship was a serious commitment. In some ways it was like being committed to a spouse because it implied high expectations of a friend. Needless to say, these high standards for friendship brought a good deal of grief to my friend who told me that he'd been disappointed in people he thought were friends for as long as he could remember. It seems evident that one's definition of friendship has a good deal to do with whether or not we are able to find and retain friends.

We often have friends who take up much of our time together talking about themselves. It's tough being with someone like this since the relationship begins to seem out of balance. A friend told me the following story about just such a relationship:

PERSONAL STORY: MAKING UP

"You have so few people who are friends as you age, you shouldn't squander them, even if they do maddening things like Jack, a friend from my days of working in Oregon. Jack can be a terrific guy, but sometimes he doesn't listen, or maybe he's not aware that you have something important to say. One day when I was in the midst of a bad time in my relationship and had some important things I wanted to share, I just got angry at him for not listening and told him off. We stopped speaking to each other for over a year. About a year later I went through a serious medical problem and wrote him to apologize. It bothered me that we'd left things as they were without trying to reconcile. This is some of what I said:

Jack:

I want to apologize for my boorish behavior last year. You have a few good friends and you should never squander them. I was in the midst of a serious illness and I felt awful when we spoke and exchanged e-mails, but that's not an excuse, just to let you know. It turns out that what I had then continued on this summer and fall and finally I had surgery but not before some damage had been done to my pancreas and liver. My local doc just missed all the signs and did pretty much nothing. I hope we can put this past us as we've done before, but if not, the apology is important and I hope you accept it in the spirit it's given.

"He wrote back a very positive e-mail saying that friends were hard to come by and you should try and keep everyone and nurture the relationship. His response made me feel a lot better although he hasn't written much since. It's OK. What I said to him originally came out of anger and it wasn't like me. I'm glad I apologized. This guy had done a lot of nice things for me. He's difficult and everyone knows it, but it diminishes me to tell people off.

"It's a lot better to try and resolve things rationally, but sometimes your emotions get in the way. Spinoza said, 'Pride and memory had an argument about something that happened in the past. Pride won the argument.' We tend to see things from our own perspective and often the little hurts become big ones when we think about them too much.

"As a poor kid when I was growing up, I had a chip on my shoulder. If anyone tried to hurt me, I'd wipe them off my list of people I cared about and they stopped existing. The inclination is still there to do the same thing I did as a kid, but I'm not a kid anymore and wiping the slate clean of everyone who hurts you leaves you with no one. Who wants that to happen? Not me."—J. B.

PERSONAL STORY: FRIENDS

The following story by a 75-year-old single woman discusses the bittersweet experiences of forming and sometimes failing to find the good friends most of us long for.

FRIENDS

Three . . . are my friends.
One that loves me.
One that hates me.
One that is indifferent to me.
Who loves me teaches me tenderness.
Who hates me teaches me caution.
Who is indifferent to me, teaches me self-reliance.

"There's an e-mail floating around in cyberspace that says, 'People come into your life for a reason, a season, or a lifetime.' When someone is in your life for a reason, it is usually to meet a need you have expressed. When they come in for a season, it's usually because your turn has come to share, grow, or learn. Lifetime relationships teach you lifetime lessons, things you must build upon in order to have a solid emotional foundation. Your job is to accept the lesson.

"When I was growing up my friends and I all lived on the same block. We would play together all day and into the night during the summer when it stayed light out until late into the evening. Life was safe back then and there were no monsters roaming the streets looking for innocent children. We played ball in a vacant lot, we jumped rope out front, and tag was popular as were marbles and jacks. There were flowers to smell, butterflies to catch, clouds to gaze into and plates of cookies in every house. We all went to the same schools and no one ever talked about what went on when we went home and the door was closed.

"The friends I made then have been coming back and forth into my life for the past 55 years, but where ever we end up we always know that the connection of growing up together is still there. We see each other at high school reunions and catch up with what's been happening in our lives with notes in the alumni association's newsletter. We may not see each other for years, but when we do get together it's as if we've never been apart.

"I've now discovered that of the people who have come into my life since then, most of them have only come into my life for a season and I wonder if the word 'acquaintance' wouldn't better describe them than 'friend.' At times I would think that I had made a really good friend, only to discover months later that they had in reality only come into my life for a reason or a season. I can't count the number of times that I've asked myself, 'What did I do wrong?' It took many years of inner dialogue to accept the fact that they were only there for a short time and I had nothing to do with them leaving. And yes, there were lessons I had to learn and pain I had to overcome. Of the lessons they were supposed to teach me, I hope I've learned them all.

"By nature I'm normally a shy person when it comes to meeting new people, and that's required some work through the years too. Now I can talk to anyone, anyplace, anytime, but I still find myself holding back a little when it comes to making a friendship. You know how it goes. You talk to someone, find out what their interests are until you find something common to share with them. It either takes off from there, or dies at the end of the conversation. I've met people that thought the same as I did on a number of subjects, but we could never be friends, the chemistry just wasn't there. And then there have been some that I would have given my eldest child to be friends with, but I wasn't worth the effort to them.

"And so it's gone through the years. I have friends from childhood that I communicate with on a regular basis, I have friends that I attend school with, I have friends that I sing with, and friends that I can just hang around with. But in the final analysis, there are three women that would be at my side, without question, should I need them. One that I that I shared a Bat Mitzvah with 25 years ago, that's Linda; one that shares my passions, that's Theresa; and the last is my youngest daughter, Rosalie, who holds me up when I falter and convinces me to keep on going.

"I lost a friend on July 4 of this year. We buried Sharon last Sunday. I looked around at the group of people at her grave site and realized along with her family and neighbors there were long-time friends and we had all added something different to her life as she had to ours.

"Rabbi Laibson read letters that had been written by members of her family, all recalling something that was special to each to them. It was very moving and I realized that while it's very important to have friends around when you're alive and crave laughter and company, it's also good to have them after you're gone. They're the ones that will smile when your name is mentioned and tell everyone within listening distance what you meant to them. They keep you alive long after your spirit has left. It's like a quote that I once read by an anonymous writer: 'Without friends you're like a book that nobody bothers to pick up.'"—G. S.

PERSONAL STORY: OLDER FRIENDS ARE THE BEST FRIENDS

The following story was told to me (the author) by my friend Jack, an 87-year-old, astonishingly healthy and vital man whom I met playing tennis a year ago. This is what Jack told me:

"I think as we age we develop more friendships than when we were younger. We have more time for friends and more need because of health problems and other issues that come up. I'm confident that the people I call friends would help me out if I had a crisis. They know I'd do the same for them.

"Our friend Jim has a serious liver ailment. He's always taken me to the doctor or hospital when I needed him to, and I've done the same for him. He's gone to Mayo in Phoenix today [about a 2-hour drive] for more tests and Bob [one of our friends] drove him down. I have a number of other people I know are my friends who have done wonderful things for me when I've asked. They do it without any hesitation.

"Older friends are different than friends we had when we younger. We depend on them more and we don't have anything to prove. We don't have the money problems we had when we were younger and we've all saved our money and have enough to live well. So there's no competition to see who's more successful or who makes the most money.

"I choose friends who are optimistic and positive about life. People who are always down don't have much to give back. I met most of my

friends at tennis and I have a core of friends my wife and I socialize
with. I certainly have more friends now, good friends, than I did
before I retired, but I have old friends and we still talk to each other.
It's true that I'm outgoing and make friends easily but I know the difference between real friends and acquaintances. I don't think I've ever
been wrong about who my real friends are.

"I once told you about being shot during a random shooting when
I was in the commercial real estate business in Los Angeles. It caused
me about six months of depression but I had friends who were supportive and in time I worked my way out of it by being productive in my job.
I think most of my friends are pretty resilient and they all believe that
life is what you make of it. You can choose to be happy or you can
choose to miserable. I choose to happy and I want to be around other
happy people.

"Happiness at my age doesn't mean that you don't have problems.
We all of have medical problems at this point in life. You [the author]
come to coffee with the guys and you know we all talk about medical
problems, but we don't let it get us down. It's what happens when
we age. But all my friends take medical problems in stride and they
get on with their lives. Me too. What else are you going to do?

"So, I'd tell the readers of your book that all the stuff you hear about
older people being unhappy and lonely doesn't apply to lots of us.
I'm 87 and every day is a new day for me. I approach each day with a
feeling that it will be special, and that I'll enjoy the company of my
friends because we'll laugh, and joke, and make each other happier
than when the day started. I see my friends for coffee almost every
day, even on a day like today when it's snowing and the roads are bad
(there are six of us having coffee and schmoozing at the St. Michael's
Hotel in Prescott, Arizona), and it just makes me happy to be together.
It's like a big happy family, in a way."

(It's snowing out in Prescott and we're about to have the worst
storm in Northern Arizona history. Jack mentions that he had to go
searching for his winter boots before he came for coffee today but they
just don't feel right. One of the guys in our Monday morning coffee
group looked down at his boots and told Jack that the reason they
didn't feel right was that he'd put them on the wrong feet. Everyone
broke up, including Jack, who thanked the guy and told him he'd
saved him from buying new boots.)

Jack continues: "You just show up for coffee and everyone is there
no matter what. The waitresses know I can't cut things and cut it for
me to make eating easier. My friend—" he nudges the guy next to

him, "always forgets to bring any money so we share breakfast. One of these days he'll remember and buy me breakfast, but it hasn't happened yet, has it?" He again nudges the fellow next to him who is hard of hearing but says that as long as Jack buys, there's no reason for him to bring money. Jack says, "You can't argue with that, but why not? I have all the money I need and I can't eat a whole breakfast, so why not share? He's my friend. That's what friends do."—J. S.

I feel the same way and drive home through the snow and slush thinking how happy I'll be to write what Jack said and to know that Jack and the others really are my friends.

SUMMARY

This chapter is about the differences between the true friends many of us long for and the more superficial acquaintances we have in our life, and how to tell the difference. The chapter includes three stories by people on their definitions of friendships and how it has affected their relationships, good and bad. Our definition of friendships is often influenced by how our parents approached our friends when we were children and how they modeled friendships in their own lives.

REFERENCES

Chen, N. (2009). "Friendship Is Important to Older Adults." Retrieved June 4, 2009 from: http://missourifamilies.org/features/agingarticles/agingfeature11.htm.

Felmlee, D., and Muraco, A. (2009). "Gender and Friendship Norms among Older Adults." *Research on Aging* 31 (3): 318–44.

Paul, M. (2005). *The Friendship Crisis: Finding, Making, and Keeping Friends When You're Not a Kid Anymore*. Emmaus, PA: Rodale Books.

Schnittker, J. (2007). "Look (Closely) at All the Lonely People: Age and the Social Psychology of Social Support." *Journal of Aging and Health* 19 (4): 659–82.

CHAPTER 9

Resolving Problems
with Children
and Family Members

INTRODUCTION

One of the more hurtful experiences older adults tell me about is the less than successful relationships they have with children and other family members. They talk of an eroding amount of contact, lack of cards or calls on birthdays, attempts to get closer or resolve problems that are ignored, and a feeling that children and brothers and sisters they loved so much early in life have turned away from them for reasons they can't understand. In this chapter, we'll look at the research on family interaction with suggestions made about how you can improve relationships—suggestions that come from my own experiences as a social worker, teacher, father, and brother to two siblings. But before I do that let's look at some of the research on family interactions with older adults.

HOW FAMILIES INTERACT

Although many of us believe that children and family members will let us down as we age, particularly when we are most in need of their involvement, Glaser and colleagues (2008) found that to the contrary, children often help out when older adult marriages dissolve or in the event of the death of a spouse. The researchers also found that although much of the current literature points to a distancing by family members if an older adult divorces, the researchers found a changing attitude toward the divorcing parent who remarries and as much help given when needed to that parent as when he or she was still married to a long-term mate.

What we *do* know is that some older adults have had troubled relationships with their children over a long period of time. This is particularly true of parents who were emotionally aloof, failed to form an attachment because of long periods of time away from their children, abused alcohol and drugs, or were physically and emotionally abusive. To think that these children will form positive attachments with their older adult parents and provide supportive help when it's needed may be unrealistic. Cyphers (1999) reports that almost two-thirds (67%) of all elder abuse is committed by adult children and their spouses. Before plans are made to heavily involve yourself with adult children and their families, you really need to evaluate the quality of your relationship with your children. If there have been unresolved problems in the past that continue on, not a few of us have sought professional help to try to find new ways of dealing with our children.

ADAPTING TO YOUR ADULT CHILDREN

In her interesting book, *Walking on Eggshells: Navigating the Delicate Relationship Between Parents and Their Adult Children,* Jane Isay interviewed dozens of older adult parents and their adult children about ways of resolving tensions and improving communications. The title refers to the fact that the people she interviewed felt as if they were walking on eggshells with one another and felt fearful that saying or doing the wrong thing would disturb fragile relationships.

From my professional experiences as a social worker helping children and parents develop better relationships, and considering Jane Isay's important work, I suggest the following ways of dealing with important relationship issues:

- **Communications.** It's important to recognize the way family members communicate with each other. Those communication patterns require you to be sensitive to each family member and not to allow others to interfere with the way you communicate with each other if it honestly works.

- **Finances.** Talk openly to your children about money, your finances, wills, trusts, and health directives. All of your children should be present. Be sensitive to everyone present so that you don't play favorites. My experience is that when everyone is together, the decisions are better and less likely to cause conflict among siblings.

- **Contact.** Stay in touch with your children by phone, e-mail, and in person. I use e-mail a lot but my daughter and I talk on the phone every week about the more important things that e-mail doesn't quite permit. We're both computer people and e-mail is a quick and easy way for us to stay in touch. If we have other things that need talking about we use e-mail to decide the best time to talk. We also try to get together at least once a month by meeting halfway between our respective homes 200 miles apart. Deciding in advance on times to talk recognizes that my daughter is far busier than I am and can't always talk when it's convenient for me.

- **Respect.** Be respectful to your children. Perhaps that's a cliché, but when I talk to my daughter I recognize that she's a highly intelligent, highly competent adult with ideas and thoughts that are always interesting to hear. She also knows a lot more about a number of technical things than I do. I always try to be respectful and appreciative of the time we spend together. Next week, on a Sunday when she's free, we're meeting halfway between our homes and having lunch together. It allows us to see each other but avoids an extra two-hour drive for either of us. We try to do that a lot. I'm always amazed by how much she knows about things I know nothing about, and I'm always appreciative of the time she takes away from her busy life to be with me. I don't want these get-togethers to feel obligatory. Rather, I'd like them to come naturally, as they usually do, whenever we discuss meeting.

- **Involvement.** Be involved but be careful about too much advice-giving. If the relationship is good, children will ask for your advice. I've been a social worker all my professional life. People seldom if ever use advice that isn't asked for. In fact, they often resent it. I know that I do, so I don't give advice. I offer suggestions when they are asked for. I've learned from my teaching career that everyone needs room to fail and that my job is to be supportive and encouraging. If people, including loved ones, don't want to use my suggestions and fail, that's their right. It's not my job to save people from making mistakes. Instead, it's my job to lovingly help them learn from their mistakes.

- **Seek Help If Needed.** If your relationship is so contentious that you can't seem to make things right with your child or children, it's always a good idea to seek professional help for good sound advice.

There are also numerous books that are written on the subject. Jane Isay's aforementioned book is just one of many good books.

- **Don't Give UP.** Don't give up on your children. To have conflict with children is a normal part of parenting. Even having a few years when things are not going well isn't uncommon, particularly during adolescence and young adulthood. We all strive to achieve independence by rebelling a bit against our parents. By staying in there, you leave the door open and sooner rather than later you may be surprised and happy to know that your adult child values you as much as you value them. So stick in there.

PERSONAL STORY: CONFLICT BETWEEN AN OLDER MOTHER AND HER DAUGHTER

"My mother and I always had a rocky, distant relationship, and when I married and became pregnant, I vowed that if I had a daughter, I would do whatever I could to make the relationship between my daughter and me better than what I had experienced with my mother.

During my pregnancy, I had a fantasy about what I hoped the relationship would be between me and the daughter I hoped to have. When I did have a daughter, Joanne, my fantasy was that not only would she and I be very close, but that she would also be educated, intelligent, beautiful and self-assured. Many of those attributes were ones I saw as those I lacked.

"As the years passed and Joanne grew, she and I were indeed quite close, and I took great pride and pleasure in our closeness. After her father and I divorced, Joanne lived with me while she attended graduate school. It was especially during those years that we had the opportunity to spend quality time together. We took long walks and stopped at our newly-found favorite coffee shop, entered 5- and 10K charity races together, went out to dinners and movies and concerts, and spent long hours simply talking. She indeed had grown into an intelligent, educated, self-assured, beautiful woman, and I was very proud to be her mother. On her wedding day, I was in tears, realizing how the fantasy I had while I was pregnant with her had been accomplished in every respect. I was overwhelmed to think how incredibly lucky I was.

"Needless to say, those years she was in graduate school could not last. Joanne started a successful career, got married, and had her own daughter. In addition to those changes, I retired from my job, remarried, and moved out of state. Inevitably, the dynamics of the relationship between Joanne and me, as I suppose should be expected, changed. As much as I know intellectually that this transition is a necessary part of life, both hers and mine, I am saddened that we have, of necessity, grown apart. Whereas previously I would have spent every other weekend at Joanne's, about an hour away, after my remarriage I spent less time there, as I now had a richer life of my own. Also, I feared that by having spent so much time there previously, I might have been turning into an annoyance.

"When I informed Joanne that my husband and I would be moving out of state, she made a comment, seemingly jokingly, that we were moving further from her and closer to my husband's daughter. The implication that this was deliberate hurt.

"Joanne and I are both now wrapped up in our separate lives, and as much as I am very happy, I also find myself wistfully thinking about how things used to be between us. I now find myself in a position I never expected—as a mother who occasionally whines about how 'my daughter never calls me.' I feel that I am the one, more often than not, reaching out, and that she is not reciprocating. I am almost always the one to pick up the phone and call, and I find myself resisting doing so because I am feeling a little angry about what I see as her neglect of me. And then I feel stupid for feeling that way.

"Joanne and I had a long talk recently about my feelings about our relationship, and she was a little defensive. Things between us seemed to be somewhat better in the ensuing weeks and months, but it didn't last.

"I try to tell myself that now, in my early sixties, I am leading a full and satisfying life and I should be grateful for that—and I truly am. And since Joanne is also leading a full, busy life, what more, I tell myself, could I ask for? But I ask for a lot—I want our closeness back, and I don't know what to do about it."—F. H.

IN-LAWS

One of the most frequent criticisms of older adults is the difficulties they experience with sons- or daughters-in-law and their parents. The reasons for these difficulties are, of course, as varied as they can be, but some common behavior that many of us find extremely annoying may be seen in the following power tactics (Family Education, 2009):

1. In-laws who are "passive-submissive." People like this usually find the most powerful person in the family hierarchy and cling

to them. They agree with everything that person says and generally contribute little if anything. They are what some people call *nebbishes*, a Yiddish word meaning they hardly exist and hide in the background.

2. In-laws who are "passive-aggressive." These people use indirect manipulation to get what they want. They often seem to go along with family decisions but inwardly resent that they are doing so. As a result, they often subtly resist and even sabotage the plans that have been made. Examples might be your in-law who doesn't want to attend a party, and so shows up an hour late, or an in-law who goes to an event she'd rather skip and then embarrasses her spouse in front of everyone.

3. In-laws who are "passive-suffering." These folks give others the responsibility for any decision or activity, but when things don't work out, they criticize the very people they've given power to.

4. In-laws who are "assertive-compromising." These folks have a position but are open to changing that position if the argument against it is a good one. These are the in-laws we usually get along with.

5. In-laws who are "assertive-controlling." These folks always want their way no matter what. Most of us avoid these in-laws and resent their insistence on always getting their way no matter how much it alienates them from the rest of the family. "Beware of assertive-controlling in-laws. Since they are terrified of feeling powerless, they usually take no prisoners in their climb to the top" (Family Education 2009, p. 1).

And then there are the spouses of our children who often seem to avoid us, dislike us for reasons we can't quite understand, seem to feel we don't accept them no matter how hard we try, believe we interfere too much in their married life, or believe we care only about our children and not about them, and so on. The list goes on but the end result is that our children seem to be lost to us and we feel hurt and confused. What should we do? Jane Angelich (2009) suggests that we use the following guidelines:

1. Respect your child and son- or daughter-in-law's boundaries. Show consideration for their busy schedules and need for privacy. Be flexible when making plans with them, keeping in mind that they have their own lives. For sure, don't show up unannounced and expect to feel welcome.

2. Try to inspire the couple by being a strong role model for them—living a rich and full life independent of them. For certain, don't put pressure on them when it comes to their children or their work but be prepared to provide information and suggestions if asked for them.

A friend told me that he'd recently seen his daughter and son-in-law and made a cardinal rule about interfering in their lives. His son-in-law teaches middle school in an urban area. The work is difficult and the pay is poor. He was venting about the job and how he often feels hopeless when he sees the many problems the kids have to deal with in their home lives that bode badly for school performance. My friend began to lecture him about taking chances and trying out some new kind of work that paid better and had fewer frustrations. In reality his son-in-law adores his job. He took over a volleyball team of seventh and eighth graders who had no uniforms and who had hardly won a game during the season and took them to the state finals. He was blowing off steam, and rather than listening and understanding, my friend lectured him, assuming that what had worked for him would work for his son-in-law. Later, he apologized for being one of those overbearing parents he always vowed he wouldn't be. It helped and he learned a good lesson. Listening and trying to understand the feelings of your children often results in better outcomes than giving unwanted advice. Or, another way of putting this is that you catch more flies with honey than you can with vinegar.

We often have problems with our adult child's in-laws that seem to mirror the concerns noted previously. Here are some suggestions for dealing with in-laws:

- They are the parents of your child's husband or wife, so they must have some good qualities. After all, they raised the individual with whom your child has chosen to share his or her life.
- Don't criticize in-laws to your child or his or her spouse. Even though they may be aware that a spouse's parents are overbearing or rude, there is a natural tendency for your child to want to protect a spouse and his or her parents.
- Pick and choose your battles. Some things are not worth starting an argument about.
- If the relationship is particularly contentious, discuss your concerns with your spouse and work out a plan to deal with it that seems logical and satisfactory to both of you.

- If that doesn't work, try talking to your in-laws directly about how you feel, e.g., "I feel hurt when you make negative comments about us." Even though it may not stop them from continuing, expressing your feelings in itself can be empowering.
- If the in-laws are receptive to the discussion (you agree to disagree about things), set some ground rules, e.g., we agree not to talk negatively about each other in front of the kids.

PERSONAL STORY: WORKING THINGS OUT WITH DIFFICULT IN-LAWS

"Our son Lawrence married a wonderful girl whom he met in college. She's just about the nicest young woman you can imagine. We think of her as our daughter. Her parents are something else. When the kids got married we had the reception at their house. They actually set up a wet bar and charged people for drinks even though we had agreed to split the cost of the reception. Their politics are so reactionary that whenever Ralph opens his mouth my husband wants to let him have it, and not in words. He says bigoted things and can hardly get through a meal without ranting about 'rich Jew bankers' who run the world and cheat the small people in the world like him. We're Jewish, so you can imagine how we feel. Our daughter-in-law has chided them in front of us and has done everything she can do to tell them how inappropriate they are, but to no avail. He thinks that what he's saying is the truth and his wife nods and agrees with him whenever he goes off on a rant.

"We just stopped seeing them, but it caused a lot of tension with our son and daughter in-law so we grin and bear it whenever we're with them, but it's tough. One day Ralph went over the line so far that Lawrence made him and his wife leave and banned them from ever coming back. I thought they would get into a fight but they left in a huff and we didn't see them again for several years. Ralph had a stroke and it took many months of rehabilitation before he was able to move around and talk. Something happened to him as a result of the stroke and instead of the mean-spirited guy he'd been, a nice older man took his place. It isn't as if he didn't remember what he'd said or done—he did—and he apologized and said how sorry he was. He'd begun having a personality change about the time we met them and it became more and more difficult to contain his rage at the world. This was a complete change over how he'd been earlier in life and even our daughter-in-law commented how he seemed to have changed when she got married. He wouldn't see a doctor and anytime anyone suggested it he'd make a snide comment about how the 'Jew' doctors only wanted your money.

"It's not easy to reconcile who he had been with who he's become but over some months Lawrence and I worked hard at it and we've begun to enjoy their company. We wonder if there was a physical reason for the change in his behavior when we first met. The best we can figure is that he'd begun drinking heavily about the time the kids got married when he lost his business. He needed to blame it on someone and who better than Jewish people? We've been scapegoated for centuries. Anyway, because we're on better terms, the kids have begun having functions where both sets of parents attend. Like doting grandparents, we can't imagine how anyone's grandkids could ever be as wonderful as ours. And I must say that having us all together and on good terms is really satisfying. Marriage is tough enough without having stress between your parents. We have a wonderful daughter-in-law and now we can see her parents as they really are and how much they had to do with who she is."—S. A.

SUMMARY

This chapter discusses our children and their spouses and in-laws and the many difficulties we often have in dealing with them. A number of suggestions are provided about effective ways of coping with in-law problems, and several stories about troubled relationships between a mother and her daughter and the parents of their daughter-in-law are provided to help the reader understand the way older people experience and try to resolve family problems.

USEFUL WEB SITES

Author unknown (2008). Retirement Influences on Marital and Family Relations. http://family.jrank.org/pages/1406/Retirement-Retirement-Influences-on-Marital-Family-Relations.html.

Avrene L. Brandt (2008). "Transition Issues for the Elderly and Their Families." http://www.ec-online.net/knowledge/Articles/brandttransitions.html.

Illene Walcott. (2008). "Older Worker, Families and Public Policy." *Family Matters*, no. 53 (Winter 1999), pp. 77–81. http://www.aifs.gov.au/institute/pubs/fm/fm53iw2.pdf.

Mary Gilly, Hope Schau, and Mary Wolfinbarger (2008). *Seniors and the Internet: Consuming Technology to Enhance Life and Family Involvement.* http://www.crito.uci.edu/noah/HOIT/HOIT%20Papers/Seniors%20and %20the%20Internet.pdf.

Sheyna Steiner (2008). "Is Retirement Different for Women?" http:// biz.yahoo.com/brn/080820/26045.html?.v=1.

REFERENCES

Allen, J. R. (2009). "Six Keys to Successful Family Communications, or 'You Think We Should Do *WHAT* with Dad?' " Retrieved February 6, 2009 from: http://www.ec-online.net/Knowledge/Articles/6keys.html.

Angelich, J. (2009). "Loving Relationships . . . from Mother-in-Law to Daughter-in-Law." Retrieved July 8, 2009 from: http://www.examiner .com/x-5473-SF-InLaw-Relationship-Examiner~y2009m5d28-Loving -relationshipsfrom-motherinlaw-to-daughterinlaw.

Carpenter, B. D., Rickdeschel, K. M. D., Van Haitsma, K. S., and Feldman, P. H. (December 2006). "Adult Children as Informants About Parents' Psychosocial Preferences." *Family Relations* 55: 552–63.

Chatzky, J. (2009). "Have an Empty Nest? 5 Tips to Better Communicate with Your Grown Kids." Retrieved February 7, 2009 from: http://www.msnbc .msn.com/id/18273795/.

Cyphers, G. C. (1999). "Out of the Shadows: Elder Abuse and Neglect." *Policy and Practice of Public Human Services* 570, 25–30.

Family Education (2009). "Five In-Law Power Tactics." Retrieved July 7, 2009 from: http://life.familyeducation.com/social-interaction/in-laws/ 48109.html.

Hershey, D. A., Mowen, J. C., and Jacobs-Lawson, J. M. (2003). "An Experimental Comparison of Retirement Planning Intervention Seminars." *Educational Gerontology* 29 (4), 339–59.

Isay, J. (2008). *Walking on Eggshells: Navigating the Delicate Relationship Between Adult Children and Parents.* New York: Flying Dolphin Press.

Nuttman-Schwartz, O. (April/June 2007). "Like a High Wave: Adjustment to Retirement." *Families in Society* 88 (2): 192–202.

Pienta, A. M. (2003). "Partners in Marriage: An Analysis of Husbands' and Wives' Retirement Behavior." *Journal of Applied Gerontology* 22: 340.

Turner, M. J., Bailey, W. C., and Scott, J. P. (1994). "Factors Influencing Attitude Toward Retirement and Retirement Planning among Midlife University Employees." *Journal of Applied Gerontology* 13: 143–56.

CHAPTER 10

Involving Loved Ones
in Retirement Decisions

INTRODUCTION

Some of the following information first appeared in a retirement book I cowrote (Glicken and Haas 2009).

In a study by Rosenkoetter and Garris (2001) of over 600 retired people planning for retirement, the researchers found that those who planned the most were the ones most involved in life after they retired. Those who reported no planning for retirement were inadequately prepared and reported that retirement was not what they thought it would be. The researchers also found that when retirement planning was done jointly with a spouse, mate, or family members that the adjustment to retirement was much better.

I doubt that people begin to think about the social and psychological aspects of retirement early in life. Retirement may seem a long way off. They *do* think about the financial aspects of retirement early because pension and 401K decisions are often stressed by employers early in a worker's career. When do people begin to think seriously about retirement? I believe it begins to happen emotionally when we first start to experience the signs of dissatisfaction and burnout with jobs and even with our careers. Although this may not lead to a specific retirement plan, it does put the option on the table and many people begin a pre-retirement dialogue with themselves and others years before they are actually ready to retire. In this chapter, the issues you might want to think about in that pre-retirement dialogue and how you might test some of your thoughts in the real world with loved ones and friends will be discussed.

ATTITUDES ABOUT RETIREMENT

How do older people anticipate the ways in which retirement will affect their lives, and differ from their working lives? Brougham and Walsh (2005) asked over 250 older employees to indicate the importance of 29 goals and whether retirement or continued work would achieve those goals. People in the study who were still working believed the following would take place after they retired:

1. Achievement would decline from 54% to 27%.
2. Contribution to the community and to the greater society would decline from 40% to 28%.
3. Creativity would increase from 21% to 47%. This might suggest that jobs are currently thought of as uncreative or that people in the survey believed they would have more time for hobbies and other creative endeavors. The researchers defined creativity as being curious, wanting to learn, and having original and novel ideas.
4. The quality of their family lives would improve from 33% to 48%.
5. Freedom would increase from 33% to 68%.
6. Finances would decrease from 84% to 16%. The researchers defined finances as the ability to maintain a comfortable standard of living and having sufficient financial reserves to provide for self and family (e.g., money for a college education for children/ grandchildren, emergencies, and health insurance).
7. Stress would increase from 28% to 41%.
8. Marriages would improve from 31% to 48%.
9. Social life and self-reliance would all decrease from high 55% to 33%.
10. Work opportunities would decrease from 81% to only 8%.
11. Participation in activities which stimulated the mind and provided an opportunity to learn new skills would decline from 58% to 35%.

ACTUAL SATISFACTION WITH RETIREMENT

1. **Overall Satisfaction with Retirement.** Smith and Moen (2004) found that 79% of over 400 retirees they sampled said they were satisfied with their lives as retirees. The Health and Retirement Study (2003), with over 18,000 subjects, found that 62% had high levels of satisfaction with retirement, while 33% said they were only somewhat satisfied, and only 5% reported dissatisfaction.

2. **Marriage Satisfaction.** When couples were asked about their satisfaction with retirement, 67% of the individual spouses said they were satisfied with retirement, while 59% of the couples surveyed said they were jointly satisfied, according to a study by Smith and Moen (2004) of over 400 retirees aged 50–72. The couples most likely to report being satisfied with retirement, individually and jointly, were those retired wives and their husbands whose wives reported that their husbands were not influential in their retirement decision.

3. **Stress and Mental Health.** Drentea (2002) analyzed data from two large national studies of retirement satisfaction with thousands of subjects. She concluded that retirement actually improves mental health because it decreases anxiety and distress often associated with work. Bakalar (2006) reports on a study of 280 socially disadvantaged men with low-level jobs who were interviewed about life satisfaction from adolescence until an average age of 75. The researchers found that happiness in retirement didn't depend on good health or having a large income in this group of men. Men who found retirement satisfying were more than twice as likely to report enjoying relationships, volunteering, and having hobbies among their favorite activities as were those who found retirement unrewarding. Men who were unhappily retired said that they occupied their lives what the researchers called "autistic activities" such as watching television, gambling, or caring for themselves.

4. **Satisfaction with Health.** In a study of satisfaction with health, Vaillant and Mukamal (2001) found that elderly people taking three to eight medications a day who were seen as chronically ill by their physicians saw themselves as healthier than their peers. A person's positive view of life can have a significant impact on the way people perceive their physical and emotional health.

This is strongly supported by a study of the physical and emotional health among a Catholic order of women in the Midwest (Danner, Snowdon, and Friesen, 2001). The study found that the personal statements written by very young women to enter the religious order predicted how long they would live. The more positive and affirming the personal statements written when applicants were in their late teens and early twenties, the longer their life spans, sometimes as long as 10 years beyond the mean length of life for the religious order, and up to 20 or more years longer than the general population. Many of the women in the sample lived well into their nineties and beyond. Of the 650 women in the study, six were over 100 years of age.

ISSUES TO THINK ABOUT WELL BEFORE YOU'RE READY TO RETIRE

WHAT DOES RETIREMENT REPRESENT?

For many of us, retirement represents the reward at the end of a long and productive life. It may be seen as an opportunity to rest and relax after many years of decidedly difficult work. For others, it may mean the ability to start new ventures and to do many of the things we always wanted to do but for which we had neither the time nor the income. And for some of us, retirement is a time to grow old with nothing to look forward to.

In a study of goals of retirement by age, Hershey and colleagues (2002) studied the way workers ranging in age from 20 to 67 thought retirement would affect them. They found that, regardless of age, subjects in the study felt strongly that retirement would increase their contact with others, increase leisure time, and lead to growth and creativity. So the first step in this pre-retirement dialogue is for you to rationally decide what you think retirement will lead to and to test it out by understanding that if you have difficulty making friends now, how will retirement magically improve that situation? The answer is, of course, that it won't. How do we know?

Vaillant and Mukamal (2001) found that your lifestyle at age 50 is a solid predictor of what it will be when you retire. If you have healthy behaviors at 50, it's likely that those behaviors will continue after you retire. If you have an unhappy marriage, are prone to depression or unhappiness, have few friends, and worry a lot, chances are that without some help, these behaviors will continue after you retire. Retirement is not a magic cure for long-held problems, and the first thing you should do is to compare those expectations for retirement with the reality of your present life. If there are areas of unhappiness or unhealthy living, it's easier to make changes before you retire, and as early as possible, than to wait until after you've retired.

An Example: John Amis, 61, is a divorced single male with a very good portfolio of investments. He is moderately happy with his job but cannot say truthfully that he likes it or that he wants to stay with it. In early retirement he sees himself having more time to do things he cannot do now because of the demands of his work and the level of fatigue he feels during the weekend. He has few friends, few special interests, doesn't think he wants to take on a second career, and admits that he gets bored easily. He feels neither happy nor unhappy at present. He's thought about retirement as something he could easily move into, since he has no ties to his current job or community.

He told me, "It's difficult for me to see myself staying in a job when I can make as much in retirement. I'd like to live someplace serene and beautiful, but I haven't thought about it much. I think about getting out of the boring life I have and hope that change will make my life better I don't think my life will be much different after I retire except for not having to work at a job I don't like. Other things, such as meeting people and keeping busy, will take care of themselves, I think. I am who I am and retirement isn't going to change that."

I cautioned him against taking early retirement because his lack of planning and thoughtful reflection made him a bad candidate for early retirement. I suggested pre-retirement workshops and planning, but he retired nonetheless. A year later he was back at another full-time job he didn't particularly like. He told me, "It beats sitting home all day watching soaps, that's for sure." Had he learned anything about retirement from the experience? "Yes, I don't have enough life skills to be retired. Work is pretty much how I spend my time. The year I spent not working was agony. I'm seeing a retirement specialist to help me plan better for those things I know I'm no good at. The retirement specialist is helping me connect with people by joining groups in town and having a better social life. It's not counseling as much as it is advice and practical help connecting with other people and social activities. He thinks when I'm ready for retirement that I should consider a retirement community because there are many activities and lots of ways to connect with people. I've checked them out and they depress the hell out of me, but then maybe I'm not ready to think seriously about retirement. I was good at saving enough money for retirement but not very good about the other stuff that goes along with it. I feel like I'm getting a handle on myself but whether it will do any good when I'm retired, I'm not sure. I still feel bored and lonely on weekends and vacations make me miserable. I guess I have a while before I'll be ready for retirement." I agree, but at least he's working on it.

How Do You Handle Free Time?

Many of us believe incorrectly that we'll handle free time well in retirement, but the way you handle free time now is a predictor of how you'll handle free time in the future. The best way to check this out is to see how long it takes for you to feel bored on vacations. Many of you take work with you to prevent boredom, and some of you cut vacations short to return to work even when it isn't necessary. Be honest with yourself about how well you handle free time. If it's a tough question because you can't get a sense of your reaction from short vacation breaks, you may want to test the waters out by taking advantage of a sabbatical and other paid leave programs available through your employer. Many companies have such programs, but often you'll need to look into them since they aren't always widely advertised. Most involve developing a plan of activities which will benefit the organization, and some may involve living elsewhere.

Universities offer sabbaticals, which permit faculty members to take up to two semesters off for renewal and more in-depth research on subjects associated with one's academic field. Often the first semester is at full pay, while two semesters off might reduce pay for the period to 50 percent. You are required to continue working for the organization a year or two for the length of the sabbatical or pay the sabbatical back, including benefits. Not only is this an excellent way to renew yourself and to do work you've wanted to do but were too busy to complete, but it's also a great way to test the waters for your ability to handle free time.

Organizations sometimes offer a phased retirement in which you have as long as five years to reduce the number of hours you work with the difference made up through use of your pension. For example, the California State University system allows faculty members to retire, receive their full pension, and teach up to a 50 percent load for five years after retirement. Many faculty members use this as a way to transition to full retirement, but it also has financial benefits since pensions may not fully cover living expenses.

An Example: One example of someone who used a sabbatical to test the retirement waters is Larry Anderson, a 59-year-old middle manager for a Kansas City software firm who liked his job but was worn out and needed a break. There was no sabbatical policy to provide him the needed time to renew himself from an extraordinary run of very demanding work assignments. Larry and his wife wanted to travel and for him to take time off from a work life that was quickly affecting his health because of the high-level of stress. His option was to resign, take his savings, and rest until he needed to find another job. In a long conversation with his wife, an alternative plan was developed which he would share with his boss.

The plan was to propose a differential-in-pay leave. Larry would find a replacement for his job who would work at a salary somewhat lower than Larry's. In some organizations, that amount would be up to half of the normal salary. Larry would advertise the position as a way to gain new experience for the short term. As an added incentive, he would offer to rent his house to the new person for a nominal fee. The house would be empty anyway, and finding a short-term renter made sense.

As an incentive to the company, Larry promised to do marketing research in his travels and to return with a comprehensive report at the end of his leave. The company agreed that Larry needed a break and agreed to pay the differential salary to the new person as long as Larry found a person suitable for the job. Because Larry was well connected, he was soon able to find an out-of-work colleague with excellent qualifications to work in Larry's place for the year of his leave. The agreement was that Larry would receive half salary and full benefits during the year and that he would then return to his position full-time. Larry's replacement would receive the other half of Larry's salary, a considerable improvement over unemployment compensation. If the replacement worked out, there would be an attempt to find him full-time work in the company, or in an allied company.

Larry spent a blissful time traveling for a year. He found himself renewed and ready to return to work with a full head of steam. His report saved the company much more than it may have lost in the arrangement, and his replacement now has a job with the company. These creative arrangements are possible in even the worst of business climates if you are willing to think through arrangements that benefit all parties involved.

This is not to say that phased retirement through sabbaticals and early retirement programs completely eliminates the need to prepare people to handle free time or make retirees more satisfied after full retirement. Reitzes and Mutran (2004) followed people in a phased retirement program for two years before retirement and two years after they retired. What they found was confirmation of Atchley's (1976, 1982) four stages of adjustment to retirement: (1) The *honeymoon period*, which is characterized as a euphoric period in which retirees relish their new freedom of time and space; (2) the *disenchantment period*, which reflects the emotional let-down as people face the reality of everyday life in retirement; (3) the *reorientation period*, which refers to the development of a realistic view of the social and economic opportunities and constraints of retirement; (4) the *stability period*, which occurs when people have achieved a certain accommodation and adjustment to retirement.

Reitzes and Mutran (2004) also found that (1) pre-retirement self-esteem and a rich social network, as well as pension eligibility, increased positive attitudes toward retirement throughout the 24-month period following retirement; and (2) retirement planning and voluntary retirement increased positive attitudes toward retirement in the initial period of retirement but not later in the first two years of retirement. After the honeymoon period wore off, retirees had to deal with the realities of retirement that weren't completely understood during their phased-in pre-retirement period.

I think the reason people go through Atchley's phases is that retirement without work is a shock. We often think of work in its least satisfying way as a chore, something to do to keep us in food and shelter, but work gives us meaning—it offers status, it helps us fill our time, and it provides, at its best, intense satisfaction and friendships. This is why the next chapter discusses some form of continued work after retirement, but work that is satisfying and even new and innovative.

FAMILY ISSUES

Retirement affects everyone in a family. For that reason you should talk over your plans with your extended family, including your friends. Many of them have stereotypes of retired living that are often not true, unrealistic, or don't apply to you. It's important that you deal with these misconceptions so that you have a supportive family and a core of understanding friends to help you move toward and into retirement. Some issues that family members may wish to discuss openly with you include the following: (1) Your children may be concerned that you will spend too much time with them. (2) Your spouse or significant other may worry that with extra time on your hands you might demand a great deal of his or her time and attention. (3) Concerns may exist over whether you will have enough money, and in the event of your death, how your estate will be dealt with and whether it will be apportioned fairly. (4) Friends may see you as being very active and wonder if you'll be able to handle the extra leisure time. These are all legitimate issues to consider and your response should be thoughtful, measured, and honest.

Nuttman-Schwartz (2007) notes the importance of involving family members in early retirement planning. The researcher writes, "The results [of his study] showed family perceptions' contribute to postretirement adjustment. Thus, in order to help the retirees to accept their retirement transition, it suggests that the pre-retirement intervention should focus on the family as a whole, especially when retirees plan their future" (p. 192). According to the author, pre-planning with family is particularly important when the retiree shows signs of loneliness and depression before retirement, because those emotional problems may continue and even worsen after retirement.

Carpenter and colleagues (2006) found that adult children sometimes know their parents' preferences for retired life but are often unaware of many important issues, particularly those issues that pertain to achieving a high quality of life. The researchers suggest that families engage themselves in discussions of later-life issues and find out parental preferences. The authors recognize that families may not have these discussions "because of time constraints, discomfort bringing up topics that imply eventual impairment, or simply because families lack the tools to have productive discussions about preferences" (p. 562). The authors suggest a family process to reevaluate and accommodate the changing needs and preferences of older adults as they consider and move into retirement. The researchers conclude by saying that "[b]ecause most children inevitably play some role in guiding the psychosocial care of their parents, it is imperative to find ways to improve their knowledge about parent preferences and values" (p. 562).

ADVICE FOR FAMILY MEMBERS

The first thing you should recognize is that the entire notion of retirement is anxiety-provoking for many people because it may suggest that productive life is over and that a gradual decline in health and life satisfaction is about to occur. It may also initiate fears about financial instability and boredom. Don't be surprised if your loved ones have fears and unrealistic expectations, or if they just don't want to talk about retirement. All these reactions are common and are increasingly important to discuss as the person moves closer to making the retirement decision. Your support can be very helpful. Calm listening and trying to understand the retiree's concerns are the best antidote to pre-retirement anxiety. Attacking ideas or perceptions or saying that you've read negative things about the decisions a loved one is considering is never a good way to show that you care or that you want to help. There is no better way to find out about retirement than reading good research-oriented articles and talking to older adults you respect who have gone through what your loved one is going through.

Early retirement is a particularly difficult decision to make since it often comes when older adults are burned out on work or have enough money saved so that work isn't really necessary. Most of the research suggests that people who retire early have issues related to boredom and are less satisfied than their later-retiring counterparts. This isn't always the case, but it's a finding to think about. What the potential early retiree might need is a break from work to get over stress and to get his or her creative juices flowing again. The best advice to loved ones considering early retirement is to tell them to keep their options open.

I recently spoke to a health care administrator who retired recently at age 62. Clearly, he was burned out over the increasingly stressful job of trying to keep a health facility afloat while hearing constant complaints from patients and doctors, and struggling with insurance companies to get bills paid. He told me he had no desire to work again and said that he was fully occupied with hiking, mountain bike riding, and seeing his grandchildren. He kept chatting long after we were finished playing tennis. I had the feeling that as burned out as he no doubt was, he had a lot more work left in him. I suggested that he keep his options open just in case he needed something to do at some point. He mulled it over and said that he had many options if he got bored and that maybe he'd pursue them. A wise decision, I thought. You don't go from running a multimillion dollar health facility to taking care of grandkids overnight without some potential for boredom.

I asked him how his children felt about his plan to see them more frequently. He said they were happy about it, hesitated, and then said he *assumed* they were happy about it but hadn't discussed it in any depth. I thought it would be a good idea if he did. He told me a week later that while his kids sounded happy about his plan to visit often, there was a subtle suggestion that it ought not be *too* often or *too* long. He was surprised and a little hurt but guessed it was better to find out now rather than later, and went on to discuss a part-time job possibility he had and how he thought maybe a couple of months of doing nothing might get him back in the mood to work again—but nothing, he added, as stressful as his former job. He told me, "The American health care system is tilting toward being broken, and trying to keep things together is a job I never want to tackle again." He also admitted that he was divorced and a bit lonely, and that maybe finding a mate was what he should do instead of spending too much time with his grandkids. He asked if I knew any eligible single women. Yes, I said, I did, and I'd chat with them first. If they wanted to follow up, I'd give them his name and they could call. Amazing what people tell you at the tennis courts.

Why would such a high-level person have such a limited retirement plan? Not having a spouse or mate to discuss his plan with is certainly one reason. When you're single, you get used to making your own decisions without consulting others. Burnout drove his retirement decision, but that's never a good motivator to retire because often when we leave the situation causing our burnout, our energy and drive return, and then what? Finally, he needed to chat about his plans in a quiet and ongoing way with his kids. He admitted that most of the talking he'd done about retirement was initiated during family reunions when people were happy and a little drunk, and that it was no place or time to talk about serious matters. I agreed.

I would also suggest that family members attend pre-retirement seminars with you. Being able to talk about the material in the seminars with family members helps process how you will approach a number of retirement issues. Even though you may not be ready to retire, attending pre-retirement seminars a year or two before you intend to retire gives you time to consider and plan for the many issues that retirement presents—where to live, whether you want to continue working, financial stability, spending more time with your children, and understanding Social Security, other pensions, and Medicare.

Hershey and colleagues (2002) found that pre-retirement seminars focusing on financial issues related to retirement had a positive impact on financial planning, but that carryover of learning often required a family member or friend to be present to reinforce what had been covered in the seminar before it would have a lasting impact.

Discussing the complex issues that affect married couples when one spouse is considering retirement, Pienta (2003) writes, "As more married couples enter their pre-retirement years, complex work and family issues will rise to the surface" (p. 355). Some of those issues include age differences in working couples in which the wife (or husband) has more years to work before retirement than the retiring spouse and how that affects retirement plans and retirement satisfaction. Another issue is that the younger working spouse will probably bring in more money than the retired spouse. Will this create problems in the relationship? Large age differences in spouses sometimes mean that the younger spouse may become a caretaker of the older spouse while they are still working, upsetting the younger spouse's retirement plans. Being together much of the time after retirement sometimes creates its own set of problems, while issues relating to money and inheritances may create considerable family antagonism. For these reasons, Pienta suggests the use of retirement counselors to help with future and ongoing issues related to retirement. Even though few people utilize retirement counselors at present (Turner, Bailey, and Scott 1994), I think it's a very good idea because specially trained retirement counselors can help resolve problems that are difficult to anticipate but seriously affect a couple.

A CASE EXAMPLE OF A FAMILY INVOLVEMENT IN A RETIREMENT ISSUE

Jane (62) and Sam (72) own a real estate agency in the southwestern part of the country. Sam has had multiple health problems over the past few years but has done well enough to function on his own without much help from Jane. Lately, however, Sam has begun to deteriorate physically, and he experiences ongoing angina attacks and difficulty breathing that requires Jane to spend a great deal of time transporting him to various doctors and hospitals, some at a distance from their home. As a consequence, their business is suffering and the commissions they should be earning are going to other agents. This financial setback has delayed Jane's retirement plans and has created animosities in the marriage where none existed before. Sam and Jane have three adult children who decided to call a family meeting and have an intervention of sorts. Sam realizes that Jane is upset with her caretaking duties, and he feels awful that Jane's retirement plans are on hold while she spends much of her time caring for him. In a lengthy conversation over several weeks, the family decided on the following plan:

1. They will set aside one day a week for a designated family member to take Sam to his appointments, see the doctor with him, and make certain that he received whatever medications or aftercare was recommended.

2. In the event of an emergency, the family will have a designated family member take Sam for medical care.

3. If that family member is unavailable and no one else is available, they will contract with a local cab company to provide immediate transportation with a family member or Jane coming to the medical facility as soon as they are available.

4. Jane will be allowed to continue earning commissions and increase their financial stability so that she can retire in three years.

5. After they retire, Sam and Jane would like to live on the beach in Mexico where they own a small condo. Because of Sam's medical problems and the uncertain availability of good medical care in Mexico, their son, a physician, will go with them to interview physicians in Mexico to see if there are good ones who will provide competent emergency medical help when needed.

6. The family will evaluate emergency medical planes to airlift Sam back to the United States for serious medical help, if needed.

7. Once assured of good medical care, Sam and Jane plan to retire in three years. Until then, Sam will help with the business to the extent his health allows.

I spoke to Jane after the family intervention. She said that the family discussions had helped resolve a situation that was creating animosity in an otherwise loving couple. Jane said, "I guess it never dawned on me that Sam would ever need someone to take care of him. He's always been an independent and energetic man, and I guess it was sort of a shock to begin realizing he was also human and as susceptible to illness as any of us. The family getting together and helping out made all the difference. Of course, we should have done this early on when Sam began to have heart problems but, like a lot of us who live busy lives, we didn't. I would tell anyone now, and I have told some of my friends, that having a plan before you run into an emergency is the best way to prevent the bad feelings I was beginning to have toward taking care of Sam. I think he's relieved as well. Since we all conferred, Sam's been feeling better and helping much more with the business. I think it's taken a load off his mind."

SUMMARY

This chapter discusses the importance of involving loved ones in your retirement decision and plans. Several studies are reported showing that children and other family members can be very involved in retirement planning and can help with difficult retirement decisions. The chapter strongly advises that pre-retirement seminars should be attended with family members so that the sometimes complex issues discussed in the seminars can be processed with loved ones. A case study was provided showing the benefits of family involvement and a retirement-related problem was included to show the positive benefits of involving one's family in decision-making.

USEFUL WEB SITES

Author unknown (2006). "Retirement Satisfaction Not Just about Income." Markham's Behavioral Health. http://behavioralhealth.typepad.com/markhams_behavioral_healt/2006/04/retirement_sati.html.

Barbara A. Butrica and Simone G. Schaner (July 2005). "Satisfaction and Engagement in Retirement." *Perspectives on Productive Aging*, no. 2. http://www.urban.org/UploadedPDF/311202_Perspectives2.pdf.

CNNMoney.com. "Planning for Retirement: Top 10 Things to Know." http://money.cnn.com/magazines/moneymag/money101/lesson13/.

E. Fouquereau, A. Fernandez, E. Mullet (2001). "Evaluation of Determinants of Retirement Satisfaction Among Workers and Retired Persons." http://findarticles.com/p/articles/mi_qa3852/is_200101/ai_n8928862.

Motley Fool. "How to Retire in Style" (a number of issues covered in a series of links related to retirement planning): http://www.fool.com/Retirement/RetirementPlanning/RetirementPlanning01.htm.

Planning Your Retirement: A number of useful links for U.S. News and World report at http://www.usnews.com/Topics/tag/Series/p/planning _your_retirement/index.html.

"Planning for Retirement: Your 'To Do' Planner for a Smooth Transition" (excellent discussion of when to do various pre-retirement activities and what they entail): http://www.todaysseniors.com/pages/planning _for_retirement.html.

U.S. Department of Labor. "Taking the Mystery Out of Retirement" (an excellent guide to retirement planning with a number of chapters of relevance): http://www.dol.gov/ebsa/publications/nearretirement.html.

Walter Updegrave (January 13, 2006). "Three Rules for Retiring Happy." CNNMoney.com at: http://money.cnn.com/2006/01/13/retirement/ updegrave_money_0602/index.htm.

REFERENCES

Atchley, R. C. (1975). "Adjustment to the Loss of Job at Retirement." *International Journal of Aging and Human Development* 6: 17–27.

——— (1982). "Retirement: Learning the World of Work." *Annals of the American Academy of Political and Social Sciences* 464: 120–31.

Bakalar, N. (April 4, 2006). "Retirement Contentment in Reach for Unhappy Men." *New York Times.* http://www.nytimes.com/2006/04/04/health/ psychology/04reti.html.

Brougham, R. R., and Walsh, D. A. (2005). "Goal Expectations as Predictors of Retirement Intentions." *International Aging and Human Development* 61 (2): 141–60.

Carpenter, B. D., Rickdeschel, K. M. D., Van Haitsma, K. S., and Feldman, P. H. (December 2006). "Adult Children as Informants about Parents' Psychosocial Preferences." *Family Relations* 55: 552–63.

Hershey, D. A., Jacobs-Lawson, J. M., and Neukam, K. A. (2002). "Influences of Age and Gender on Workers' Goals for Retirement." *International Journal of Aging and Human Development* 55 (2): 163–79.

Nuttman-Schwartz, O. (April/June 2007). "Men's Perception of Family During the Retirement Transition." *Families in Society* 88 (2): 192–202.

Pienta, A. M. (2003). "Partners in Marriage: An Analysis of Husbands' and Wives' Retirement Behavior." *Journal of Applied Gerontology* 22: 340.

Prince, M. J., Harwood, R. H., Blizard, R. A., and Thomas, A. (1997). "Social Support Deficits, Loneliness and Life Events as Risk Factors for Depression in Old Age: The Gospel Oak Project VI." *Psychological Medicine* 27: 323–32.

Reitzes, D. C., and Mutran, E. J. (2004). "The Transition to Retirement: Stages and Factors That Influence Retirement Adjustment." *International Journal of Aging and Human Development* 59 (1): 63–84.

Rosenkoetter, M. M., and Garris, J. M. (2001). "Retirement Planning, Use of Time, and Psychosocial Adjustment." *Issues in Mental Health Nursing* 22 (7), 703–22.

Smith, D. B., and Moen, P. (2004). "Retirement Satisfaction for Retirees and Their Spouses: Do Gender and the Retirement Decision-Making Process Matter?" *Journal of Family Issues* 25: 262.

Turner, M. J., Bailey, W. C., and Scott, J. P. (1994). "Factors Influencing Attitude Toward Retirement and Retirement Planning among Midlife University Employees." *Journal of Applied Gerontology* 13: 143–56.

Vaillant, G. E., and Mukamal, K. (2001). "Successful Aging." *American Journal of Psychiatry* 158 (6): 839–47.

CHAPTER 11

Work and Volunteering after Retirement to Increase Friendship Pools and Meet Potential Mates

INTRODUCTION

As people retire, they often decrease their social contacts by no longer working or finding other avenues to meet and interact with potential friends and mates. What should people do who are either considering retirement or are retired but worry about loneliness and lack of social contacts?

According to Zedlewski and Butrica (2007), research evidence increasingly shows that older adults who regularly work after retirement enjoy better health and live longer, thanks to stimulating environments and a sense of purpose. Calvo (2006) found that paid work for older adults improves health. Tsai and colleagues (2005) followed a sample of early retirees for 30 years and found that they died earlier than workers who retired later. Dhaval and colleagues (2006) found that complete retirement without work decreases physical and mental health.

The reasons why work improves health is that it increases cognitive activity, exposure to stimulating environments, and social interactions (Kubzansky, Berkman, and Seeman 2000), enhances social status (Thoits and Hewitt 2001), and offers greater access to social, psychological, and material resources (Wilson 2000). Some work-related activities help older adults develop knowledge and skills which boost their self-images and mental outlooks (Harlow-Rosentraub, Wilson, and Steele 2006).

Once older adults reach age 65, most will opt for retirement (Ekerdt 1998). Although some individuals move from full-time work to full-time leisure, a substantial number remain in the labor force after they leave their career jobs (Hansson, DeKoekkoek, Neece, and Patterson 1997). Many of these working "retired" adults are in "bridge-type jobs," which help them transition from long-term career positions to total retirement (Feldman 1994; Mutchler, Burr, Pienta, and Massagli 1997). Bridge jobs may be part-time work, self-employment, or temporary work and often involve a combination of fewer hours, less stress or responsibility, greater flexibility, and fewer physical demands (Feldman 1994). Bridge jobs offer possible remedies to older adults who are concerned about their financial security and to employers who face a labor shortage.

Because of downsizing, employers have been offering incentives to encourage or force costly older workers into early retirement so that many older adults have left the labor force before reaching retirement age ("Business: The Jobs Challenge," 2001). By the late 1990s, early retirements accounted for more than 80 percent of total retirements (Seymour 1999). A significant number of these early retirees participated in some form of bridge employment (Feldman 1994).

Ulrich and Brott (2005) studied the strategies used by retirees to transition into bridging jobs. The following themes emerged: (1) The majority of the participants planned for their financial future but did not consider what they wanted to do after they retired, nor did they take advantage of their community's career and job search resources. (2) Some individuals did not have to start over again because they were able to build on their past career experience, marketable skills, reputations, and personal skills. (3) Participants discovered that a bridge job sometimes introduced unwanted changes, such as lower pay, lack of career advancement, difficulties in forming close work relationships, separation from former career field, and loss of responsibilities. (4) Without sufficient planning or reaching out to available resources, many participants found it difficult to switch to a new career. They had a hard time moving into a new job if the job titles did not match their long-term career titles or if they defined their occupational field too narrowly. (5) Many did not fully investigate a job opportunity before they accepted employment and were disappointed after a period of time on the job. (6) Participants were reluctant to move into new jobs because they lacked the appropriate technological skills or they questioned their ability to learn these new skills. (7) Taking employment-related tests was viewed as an unpleasant experience for these older adults. (8) At the end of their long-term career or during their transition to a bridge job, many participants speculated that their careers and their transition efforts were affected by subtle age discrimination, such as younger employees questioning their capabilities. (9) Regardless of these challenges, participants greatly benefited from their bridge jobs. They credited their bridge jobs with making them feel better about themselves, giving them a more balanced life, and helping them enjoy their work. They also felt better about themselves because they continued to learn, made a difference to others, demonstrated their competency, and felt healthy.

An Example: Barbara Fender, 66, a Palm Springs social worker, thought that she was about as burned out as she could be from a demanding job in child protective services. She and her husband (a physician in private practice) thought about retirement as a way to reduce the stress in their lives through travel and personal growth, but a year of complete retirement from work suggested that she was not ready to stop working. When her employer asked to her return to work part-time, she jumped at the chance and is now very happy working two days a week.

I asked her why she thought retirement would be so much better than work. She told me, "This may sound strange coming from someone who works with people and knows a lot about human behavior, but we were so caught up in our careers and the stress from our jobs that we never really thought about retirement as anything but a respite from stress. We thought we'd be older than we actually are. I mean that we thought we'd feel old when in fact we feel young. We thought we'd have health problems at age 65, but thank God we both are very healthy. We thought travel would be glamorous and exciting and it was—for maybe a month—and then it just became boring. We should have taken long trips, or worked part-time, or done something to test out how we dealt with free time, but we didn't.

"The reality is that neither one of us likes a lot of free time and going back to work part-time has been wonderful. I work the first two and a half days of the week and John works the second two and a half days of the week so we have what feels like a normal work week. We were getting into each other's hair and it was annoying. Now we feel grateful to have each other evenings and weekends, and we plan trips and have our dreams, but they're a lot more realistic. I would say that a reality check should be done throughout your adult life to check out your thinking about retirement. Be honest, because we weren't and it led to a very troubled and unhappy year for us until we went back to work."

WHAT TO DO WHEN WORK
BECOMES UNPLEASANT

Older workers often have little choice in whether they continue working full-time. As Mor-Barak and Tynan (1993) point out, "Despite this interest in continued employment by employers and older adults, older workers are more likely to lose their jobs than younger workers in instances such as plant closings and corporate mergers (Beckett 1988)" (p. 45). The authors go on to say that many businesses can't or won't deal with life events faced by older workers such as "widowhood and caring for ailing spouses, and as a result many older workers are forced to retire earlier than planned" (p. 45).

Writing about the loss of work and its impact on older men, Levant (1997) says that as men lose their good-provider roles, the experience results in "severe gender role strain" (p. 221) which affects relationships and can be disruptive to the point of ending otherwise strong marriages. Because older adults are more likely to lose high-level jobs due to downsizing and age discrimination, social contacts decrease and many otherwise healthy and motivated workers must deal with increased levels of isolation and loneliness. Schneider (1998) points out that many of us are workaholics and when work is taken away or jobs are diminished in complexity and creativity, many older adults experience a decrease in physical and mental health. And while early retirement is thought to be a way to achieve the good life at an early age, the experience is a complex and even emotionally draining one, in which older adults who are financially able to retire often have little ability to handle extra time, have failed to make sound retirement plans, and find out quickly that not working takes away social contacts, status, and a way to organize time.

For many healthy, work-oriented and motivated older adults, volunteer and civic roles are not at all what they are looking for. They want to continue to work, to contribute, and to receive the financial and social status and benefits related to work. A current recession with high unemployment and loss of investment income because of the economic crash of 2008 suggests that the American workplace will see many older workers continue to work well into their seventies and beyond. The fact that Social Security has a benefit scale based on birth date will make it unlikely for many workers currently in their forties and fifties to retire early. This, of course, also has negative ramifications for workers who have worked at physically and emotionally demanding jobs and have experienced physical and emotional deterioration.

In an analysis of the impact of paid work and formal volunteerism, Zedlewski and Butrica (2007) found that numerous studies supported the finding that work and formal volunteering improved health, reduced the risk of serious illness and emotional difficulties such as depression, and improved strength and cognitive functioning, while full retirement without work and early loss of jobs increased the probability of illness and emotional difficulties. Clearly, having something of value to do after retirement keeps older adults healthy and emotionally engaged with the world around them.

> **An Example:** Jake Larson is someone who likes his job and has no plans to retire early. "I'm 68," he told me, "and I still feel a high when I go to work. I'm well taken care of financially and my wife keeps telling me we could see the world instead of my continuing to work, but to be truthful, I don't really want to see the world and she knows it. I like the folks I work with and the work is fun. I get razzed a lot about being too old to do the job but everyone knows how good I am at it. I see a lot of my friends who retired early and stopped working full-time before they were ready and they're miserable. They didn't like their jobs and I told them that maybe doing something else would make the difference, but now they work at part-time jobs that pay next to nothing. One of them greets people at Wal-Mart. He's a smart guy who was a very successful appraiser, but unhappy in his work, and now he greets people. I know that he hates it. He quit his job because he was burned out and wishes he was back at it, but with the current housing market in shambles he can't find anything in the appraisal field. I think planning for work after you retire is a necessity, and if you like your job and you can keep working, I'd recommend that people do it. When I actually *do* retire, we'll be very comfortable financially. Just working these few years past 65 has made a real difference in our savings."

PERSONAL STORY: WORKING AFTER RETIREMENT

"I drive two hours each way from my home to teach courses each semester at a major university. Driving down the mountain from my house in the Arizona backcountry is stunning. You go by Dead Bug Wash, Black River Canyon, Horse Thief Canyon, and vistas that make you want to hug the scenery. It's a little like you felt as a kid watching a John Wayne movie only you have a cup of coffee with you and you're listening to a CD by Alison Krauss so beautiful and touching that you want to play it for your students when you see them.

"On the way to class I stop at the factory outlet stores outside of Phoenix for coffee and find myself buying clothes I need but would never buy because . . . well, because I never thought of myself as someone who wanted to look especially good for others. Academics are just not into clothes. Now that I have some decent clothes to wear I find myself enjoying the pleasure of dressing well (sort of well, anyway). I've lost a lot of weight so the pleasure is that much better.

"Once I get to campus I have a Starbucks coffee in the library, check my e-mail before class, and notice the serious working-class students at a bank of computers. School is no picnic and most of them work second jobs, sometimes full-time, to pay their tuition. It's hard to think that many of them have parents affluent enough to pay their university expenses, yet here they are. It makes me feel optimistic about the future to see such hard-working young people.

"I go to my classes, and while I don't feel I'm as good as I could be because I'm a bit tired from the drive, the students are happy to see me. They've begun to realize that I spend much more time with them than their full-time teachers and that I respond to e-mails and grade their papers very quickly. Several students have told me they never get responses from their teachers, and when I respond as soon as they send an e-mail, it's startling, but in a nice way.

"To help me remember lecture material I audiotape my lectures, play a bit of what I've recorded in class, and then expand on the material. It seems like a good approach and the students don't appear to mind. I record my lectures the day before classes in the morning when I'm fresh and then listen to them in the car while driving to teach. Many times I tell jokes when I record lectures and find myself laughing at the puns and bad jokes I tell students.

"I've become very good at using the academic Internet program Blackboard and spent a few days with the help of an IT person learning the mysteries and benefits of that great teaching tool. Because of the long drive, I've decided to offer the occasional Internet class so that certain assignments and examinations can be done online. The students like the freedom and their work is much improved.

"I make a paltry sum of money for teaching, but the money goes for the frivolous things I never felt comfortable buying before: clothes, a new tennis racquet, better tennis shoes, hiking gear so I can hike these beautiful Arizona mountains, particularly the many hiking trails in and around Sedona. I feel rich with the extra money, and it makes me very generous. I figure that what I make is play money because I get such pleasure from it, so why shouldn't other people benefit?

"I've tried to volunteer but I'm still tied to the notion that you should be paid for your labor if you are to be valued. I've begun consulting for a new university in my town that will offer a first year of college to young adults in recovery. The money is nice, the work is very interesting, and I feel valued. Between all of that and the books I write, my plate is full. I have time to work out, to hike, and to go to political and social events, but the work sustains me and makes me feel that, although I'm retired, I'm really still working: for myself and not the large organizations that treat older adults so badly. It's a wonderful feeling, one I dreamed of when I was working full-time at stressful jobs.

"I think work is a necessary part of the aging process. I don't think volunteer work has the same emotional value as paid work, but that's me. And it's not the amount of money you make, it's the fact that you can now focus on what you love doing. There is no amount of money that can equal the feeling of complete independence to pick and choose what excites you.

"It isn't growing old that worries us older people, it's the fear we'll grow old and be bored. To have work that still excites you, that's one of the best rewards. That, and someone who loves you without reservation."—M. D. G.

SUMMARY

This chapter about work and volunteering after you retire encourages older adults to understand that even though we may be burned out on our jobs when we reach retirement age, many people continue to work part-time at jobs that keep them engaged and occupied without the stress of full-time jobs. The chapter also notes the research that indicates older adults who work and volunteer have fewer health problems, are more satisfied with their lives, and help them improve their social lives by meeting people at work. A story at the end of the chapter describes the positive results of working part-time and the joy the writer gets from working with younger people.

USEFUL WEB SITES

CNNMoney.com. "Planning for Retirement: Top 10 Things to Know."
   http://money.cnn.com/magazines/moneymag/money101/lesson13/.
"Planning for Retirement: Your 'To Do' Planner for a Smooth Transition"
   (excellent discussion of when to do various pre-retirement activities and
   what they entail): http://www.todaysseniors.com/pages/planning_for
   _retirement.html.
Planning Your Retirement: A number of useful links for U.S. News and
   World report at: http://www.usnews.com/Topics/tag/Series/p/planning
   _your_retirement/index.html.
U.S. Department of Labor. "Taking the Mystery Out of Retirement" (an excellent guide to retirement planning with a number of chapters of relevance):
   http://www.dol.gov/ebsa/publications/nearretirement.html.
Walter Updegrave (January 13, 2006). "Three Rules for Retiring Happy."
   CNN.Money at: http://money.cnn.com/2006/01/13/retirement/upde
   grave_money_0602/index.htm.

REFERENCES

Beckett, J. O. (1988). "Plant Closing: How Older Workers Are Affected."
   Social Work 33: 29–33.
"Business: The Jobs Challenge" (July 14, 2001). *The Economist* 360: 56–57.
Calvo, E. (2006). "Does Working Longer Make People Healthier and
   Happier?" *Work Opportunities for Older Americans*, Series 2. Chestnut
   Hill, MA: Center for Retirement Research, Boston College.
Dhaval, D., Rashad, I., and Spasojevic, J. (2006). "The Effects of Retirement
   on Physical and Mental Health Outcomes." NBER Working Paper
   12123. Cambridge, MA: National Bureau of Economic Research.
Ekerdt, D. (1998). "Workplace Norms for the Timing of Retirement."
   In Schaie, K., and Schooler, C. (eds.), *Impact of Work on Older Adults*.
   New York: Springer: 101–23.
Feldman, D. C. (1994). "The Decision to Retire Early: A Review and Con-
   ceptualization." *Academy of Management Review* 19: 285–311.
Hansson, R. O., DeKoekkoek, P. D., Neece, W. M., and Patterson, D. W.
   (1997). "Successful Aging at Work—Annual Review, 1992–1996: The
   Older Worker and Transition to Retirement." *Journal of Vocational
   Behavior* 51: 202–33.
Harlow-Rosentraub, K., Wilson, L., and Steele, J. (2006). "Expanding Youth
   Service Concepts for Older Adults: Americorps Results." In Wilson, L.,
   and Simson, S. (eds.), *Civic Engagement and the Baby Boomer Generation:
   Research, Policy and Practice Perspectives*. New York: Haworth Press:
   61–84.

Kubzansky, L. D., Berkman, L. F., and Seeman, T. E. (2000). "Social Conditions and Distress in Elderly Persons: Findings from the MacArthur
Studies of Successful Aging." *Journals of Gerontology: Psychological Science*
55b (4): 238–46.

Levant, R. F. (1997). "The Masculinity Issue." *Journal of Men's Studies* 5 (3):
221–29.

Mor-Barak, M. E., and Tynan, M. (January 1993). "Older Workers and the
Workplace: A New Challenge for Occupational Social Work." *Social
Work* 38 (1): 45–55.

Mutchler, J. E., Burr, J. A., Pienta, A. M., and Massagli, M. P. (1997). "Pathways
to Labor Force Exit: Work Transitions and Work Instability." *Journal of
Gerontology: Social Sciences* 52b: S4–S12.

Schneider, K. J. (1998). "Toward a Science of the Heart: Romanticism and
the Revival of Psychology." *American Psychologist* 53 (3): 277–89.

Thoits, P. A., and Hewitt, L. N. (2001). "Volunteer Work and Well-Being."
Journal of Health and Social Behavior 42 (2): 115–31.

Ulrich, L. B., and Brott, P. E. (December 2005). "Older Workers and Bridge
Employment: Redefining Retirement." *Journal of Employment Counseling*
42: 159–70.

Wilson, J. (2000). "Volunteering." *Annual Review of Sociology* 26: 215–40.

Zedlewski, S. R., and Burtrica, B. A. (December 2007). "Are We Taking Full
Advantage of Older Adults' Potential?" The Retirement Project: Perspectives of Productive Aging. *The Urban Institute* 9, 1–8.

CHAPTER **12**

Where You Live as an Older Adult Can Make a Difference

There are a number of wonderful places to live after you retire where you can meet interesting older adults and where friendships and romances often flourish. If you can afford it, moving to a new community with a milder climate or a lower cost of living is always a consideration. So is staying put and spending that part of the year with bad weather somewhere else. In this chapter we will consider the pros and cons of moving, staying where you are, retirement communities, and what the experts say about the best places to retire that offer a lively social and cultural scene and many opportunities for meeting people.

RETIREMENT COMMUNITIES

There are a number of excellent retirement communities in the United States. It's not my purpose to tell you which one is best for you (I've included a Web site with the 100 best planned communities at the end of the chapter, but I don't endorse it and list it only for your convenience), but I *will* discuss issues to consider in selecting a community and some information about retirement communities from the research literature to help you select the one that's best for you. As Streib (2002) writes, "Retirement communities can be havens for many older people because they offer services, transportation, security, activities, social activities, neighborliness, that many older adults want and need" (p. 4).

A retirement community is often defined as one where you or your spouse must be 55 or over. The reality is that younger families sometimes live in retirement communities with their older parents. Some communities limit their stay to 60 days, but I hear it's a rule that's not often enforced. You need to check with the community administration if you consider this to be a problem and do some drive-bys to see if there are children out in any numbers in the late afternoon and early evening.

Retirement communities often have an amazing number of activities including golf, tennis, swimming, gyms, hiking trails, clubs of every type, dances, trips, and social events that help you meet other residents. You will be charged a fee paid to the homeowners association (HOA) for all of these extra activities. It's usually fairly inexpensive ($100–200 or less a month), but beware of new communities where the builder supports the HOA to keep fees low. There are communities every day that have to substantially raise HOA fees because the builder has only committed to subsidizing the community for a limited period of time, or because the builder goes into bankruptcy. Fees then go up dramatically. Be sure to find out the stability of fees and repair and renovation projects that may increase fees, such as swimming pool, roof, or tennis court renovations. In some communities HOA dues cover repairs of the outside of your home or condo. If massive repairs of roofs are needed it can dramatically raise your HOA fees or result in a large one-time assessment.

Retirement communities sometimes have problems with management companies who do a poor job, so look at the management company's record before you select a community. If management companies change often it could mean an overly demanding or intrusive HOA board of directors or a poorly functioning board that provides little oversight. Both spell trouble.

Lapsley (2001) found that residents of retirement communities with a need to dominate and control others sometimes gravitate to important leadership positions where they tend to enforce rigid rules that are very annoying to others. He writes, "The primary pattern of over-controlling is seen in the exploitation of leadership positions in community organizations. ... Some over-controllers in leadership roles are also quite vindictive, seeking retribution or revenge (unlimited 'payback') against those whom they perceive to have slighted them" (p. 446). It's important to determine if this is true of a board of directors in a retirement community you may want to live in. You should also find out how long people serve on boards, and whether there are ways to oust particularly difficult people. As Streib (2002) points out, "The marketing programs of retirement communities never mention that a variety of disagreements may arise and some of these may take on considerable importance" (p. 6).

A friend of mine told me about her gated retirement community where the HOA is run by former executives of corporations who try to control every aspect of community life because they haven't transitions from work to leisure time. Her husband was playing tennis on the retirement community's courts when one of the HOA directors came running out onto the court and demanded that the players show evidence that they lived in the community. They were both residents of the community for more than 10 years, knew the fellow, and got into a protracted argument about why he had disrupted their game. These kinds of problems are sometimes commonplace, so knowing about them beforehand can save a good deal of unhappiness later.

One of the ways retirement communities are able to offer fairly low rates for homes is that the basic homes without views are reasonably inexpensive, but premiums are charged for better lots. These premiums may increase the price of a home from $5,000 to $100,000 or more. A basic lot may have a lovely view of the side of someone's house and the roofs of others. There is also the issue of upgrades that can be particularly expensive and unnecessary, or that can be done privately for less money. What may begin as an inexpensive house can escalate into something beyond your means, so have a financial plan and stick to it.

Not everyone likes to be around older people all of the time. People in retirement communities tend to talk a lot about their health. If you find health talk boring or depressing, retirement communities may not be for you. Some communities have an average age that is considerably older than you are. You may want to find this out if you prefer to be around people closer to your age. There is talk about people increasingly forming neighborhoods with others who are like them in political leanings and social beliefs. I think this is true, and speaking personally about the community in which I live, often mentioned as a top 10 place to retire, the deeply conservative and sometimes bigoted beliefs of some retirees here can be a major annoyance. You should try to get a sense of the social and political leanings of the people in the community and find out if there are clusters of people with whom you are more likely to interact. It may be that the community appeals to you but that you find it difficult to form close friendships or intimate relationships because of social and political schisms.

To overcome political and social differences, many organizations exist that offer support for political and social views. In my community we have very active Republican and Democratic county organizations that offer socially, politically, and intellectually stimulating events. The American Association of University Women is very active and has lectures, book clubs, socials, and other events that bring a number of older men and women together. I happen to be a member of AAUW and I can tell you that in my chapter, men are welcome. No one asks for evidence that you've completed your degree or even gone to college. I've gone to several of their functions and found them fun, stimulating, and very friendly. We have a number of churches in town that offer singles and couples the opportunity to come together for fellowship and community activities. The Unity Church, with which I'm familiar, is a good example of a singles friendly place to meet people. The local synagogue also has stimulating and numerous social events.

Check out the community when the weather is at its worst. There is nothing like being in Sun City, Arizona in the summer when it's 118-degrees, the humidity is high from the summer monsoon rains, and the streets are absolutely vacant to give you a sense of the other side of desert living—the side you won't see during the beautiful desert winters. Some people take extended vacations or stay in retirement communities for a week or two to decide whether it's for them. I think this is a very good idea. Many retirement communities have inexpensive furnished rentals for this exact reason.

Don't be fooled by retirement communities that advertise low taxes. Many states with no income tax make up for it with high property and sales taxes. Texas, which has no income tax, may charge a 2.5–3.5 percent property tax on the assessed value of a home. For a home with a moderate assessed value of $250,000, that could mean a property tax as high as $8,750 a year. Communities in some states have added an additional city and county sales tax to an existing state sales tax which can bring the tax up to 8–10 percent or more on nonessential items such as clothing, cars, and any non-food or medication purchase. Phoenix now charges a 2 percent sales tax on food on top of county and state sales taxes. Sales taxes are regressive in that people with less income pay a much greater proportion of their income than more affluent people. This is particularly true of retirees on fixed incomes. It is also true that you get what you pay for. States with low taxes are often service-poor in many areas that are essential to older adults, including public transportation, health care, and adult education.

Finally, a retirement community should have available medical services nearby. Some new communities don't. This can present a major problem for the retiree who doesn't want to drive long distances, has problems navigating urban freeways, or has health problems that require immediate care. The same is true of other services such as shopping. I especially like communities that have nearby shopping that is easily available by cart or shuttle. Given the price of gas, driving a long distance to shop can wreak havoc on your budget.

BEST COMMUNITIES FOR RETIREES

Many national magazines have articles each year listing the best places to retire. I am always surprised to find on this list places where it's cold and the weather is miserable much of the year. I don't know why such a community is listed, but you're welcome to read these lists and even visit the communities cited to see for yourself. I find it hard to understand how lists can change each year and suspect that the articles are written with less than stellar research. Frankly, the only way to find out about a place is to spend time there. My hometown of Prescott, Arizona was one of *Money Magazine*'s top five places to retire in 2006. It's a great place, but not without its flaws. You'd have to live here a while to know that we have an extreme doctor shortage and that the average age in the county we live in is 60, which means that a large number of older people with medical problems tax an already weak medical system. Winters are cold—we do get snow and sleet—and the summers are hot and wet. During spring and fall we occasionally have forest fires and back-burning by the Forest Service that pollutes the air. Therefore, if you have asthma, it's not a good place to live.

Retirees in Prescott are very politically conservative, which makes political conversations difficult if you happen to be more liberal. Nobody would call Prescott the cultural hub of the country or, for that matter, Phoenix, a two-hour drive away. It's nice to see so much natural beauty, but sometimes you hunger for a cultural event after the cowboy storytellers at the Palace Bar begin to grow stale. It's also a complacent place and more than a few people have told me that they've lost their desire to travel and explore because Prescott is just too comfortable. I can vouch for that.

On the other hand, property taxes are fairly low, cost of living is moderate, there are 450 miles of hiking trails in the county through some incredibly beautiful country, and housing is still relatively inexpensive. There are numerous free events on the Court-house Square in downtown Prescott every summer weekend. We have a very nice Costco where there are no lines, and a surprisingly large number of national stores for such a small community. Restaurants are plentiful, people are warm and friendly, and truth be known, I wouldn't trade it for anywhere else. Well, maybe for a condo on the southern California coast or a chalet in Aspen.

Even with the best of information, adjusting to a new community is a personal thing. You find people who complain about our community and everything I think is good about it. I tend to think of them as mal-contents but when you listen to them closely you hear that it's a lonely place for singles, that it's too dominated by politicians looking out for their own self-interest, and that it's not progressive enough in ways that help older adults with their needs. Like much of the Southwest, public transportation is inadequate to nonexistent, and the prevalence of a state legislature that passes bills to permit guns in restaurants and on university campuses makes you wonder if they still live in the time of the O. K. Corral.

The point is that what's wonderful for you may be awful for some-one else. You can read the lists of best retirement communities and look, but don't take anyone's word for it. Be an active and skeptical consumer. As Pullium Weston (2008) writes, "Every location has its drawbacks, a point that's often missed by those dreaming of a brand new life in a new place. Those who move to escape their problems will probably find their issues migrated with them; as the saying goes, 'Wherever you go, there you are.' Anyway, if there were a real Shangri-La, we'd all move there and wreck it with congestion" (p. 1).

STAYING PUT

People over 65 are much less likely to move than younger people. Home is where one has memories of family, where it's comfortable and probably less expensive, and where it's close to friends, your doctor, and your handyman. You have a sense of belonging to a com-munity you have long-term ties to that may be missing when you move to a new community. Furthermore, your family is probably close by and staying put is a lot less stressful than moving, an experi-ence that may be so stressful that many people stay put so they can avoid it altogether. Streib (2002) points out that on the face of it, retirement communities have a strong attraction for many older adults. He wonders why more older adults don't move from their homes after retirement and responds by saying, "A major reason is that 'aging in place' has certain psychological benefits. It is easier for the person to remain in a familiar, comfortable place. Moving involves making difficult choices of reducing one's possessions that have been collected over a lifetime" (p. 4).

Many retirees consider living overseas because the cost of living is cheap, but on close examination they discover that a low cost of living may be offset by travel costs, lack of good medical care, and security issues. I know Mexico very well, and ads saying that you can live on a shoestring in Mexico are highly misleading and often untrue. In many ways Mexico is just as expensive and, in some instances, more expensive than the United States, and laws we take for granted are often not available to protect American homebuyers.

These are all good reasons to consider staying put when you retire, but it doesn't mean you can't or shouldn't explore other areas of the country, or even live elsewhere part of the year. Many people rent in warmer areas of the country during cold weather months and find that living in several places where they can get the best of the weather all year is ideal. Renting opens the door to living in many different places and exploring this beautiful country of ours. And it's also reasonable. There are a number of Web sites where you can find good vacation or monthly rentals, and there are opportunities to house-swap. At the end of the chapter I provide a few Web sites you might want to take a look at.

PERSONAL STORY: MOVING
TO A NEW COMMUNITY

"Linda and I met when I was about to turn 65 and she was about to turn 60. I'm a retired university professor and Linda was an attorney working for a large international law firm in Los Angeles. We began dating while I was renting a condo in Palm Springs and she lived in West Los Angeles. After a few months of commuting, I was spending more and more time with her. We thought it was silly and expensive to maintain two homes, and seven months after we met I moved into her condo in West Los Angeles.

"Both of us are from the Midwest and neither of us much liked Los Angeles, but we love the West and wanted to retire there. We spent the next year and a half using every opportunity we had to check out potential places to retire. When my daughter graduated from the University of Arizona, we checked out Tucson and Las Cruces, New Mexico, two places experts suggest are good places to retire. We found Tucson much too hot and spread out and Las Cruces a bit too small and isolated. We also spent three days in Boise, Idaho, a place I'd lived for a year, but couldn't find affordable housing near the center of the city. We also found it much more congested than it had been three years earlier. We spent a weekend visiting friends of Linda's in Portland, and found it a great place to live but also dreary and wet. We looked at communities in California such as San Luis Obispo, a wonderful place, but it was expensive beyond comprehension. We were pretty sure we wanted to live in a smaller community, but one with amenities, which was also safe and had good weather and a local college. We also wanted to live close enough to a big city so that we could have good medical care if we needed something beyond the expertise of the local community, travel on less expensive flights, and enjoy the benefits of urban life without having to deal with the liabilities.

"I knew about Prescott from my days of teaching at ASU in Tempe. When we finally went to Prescott on what I called one of our 'scouting trips,' we spent three days with an excellent real estate agent we'd found online, couldn't find a house we liked, but found the community very appealing. We originally went in August when Prescott can be very warm and wet but found that it didn't bother us. We returned in February of the next year, feeling some pressure to find something and sell Linda's condo before the real estate bubble burst in Los Angeles. Our real estate agent sent us a number of homes to look at on the Internet before we came. Fortunately, we found an exceptional house at a fair price that looked very comfortable and appealing at a fraction of the cost in Los Angeles. Linda was able to sell her condo before the bubble burst completely and made a nice profit. We moved to Prescott in May 2007 and like it in ways that only people who have lived in congested and impersonal places can understand.

"Do we miss the big city? Not a bit. Phoenix is big enough. I drive down once a week to teach at Arizona State University and enjoy the day but that's enough big city life for me. Is Prescott too small? No. I joined the local tennis club, play often, and have made some great friends, some of them a lot younger than I am. I stay very busy. Are there other places I might have found that I might like better? Perhaps, but that's for another day. Right now I'm content, busy, happy and healthy. What more could anyone my age ask for?"—M. D. G.

SUMMARY

This chapter discusses the issue of where to live after you retire. Most people stay in their homes or move nearby to be close to extended family. They also have the convenience of keeping physicians and other professionals with whom they've worked with for long periods of time. For those of you who want the many benefits of retirement community living, spending time at the community of choice during bad weather parts of the season can help you decide where to live, and so can speaking to as many members of the community as possible to find out if you'll have the social life you desire. Other considerations include closeness to doctors and shopping. Since retirement communities may be a distance from both, this is an issue that shouldn't be ignored. Finally, while retirement communities have many people, not all of them are compatible. Be sure to get a sense of whether you'll have a rich social life and opportunities to meet people and stay active. You can only do this by spending a bit of time looking for the right community and meeting people before you make this decision.

USEFUL WEB SITES

America's Top 100 Best Master-Planned Retirement Communities: http://www.retirenet.com/top100/.
Bill Ahern. "Low Tax States? Think Again": http://www.heartland.org/Article.cfm?artId=166.
CNN.Money.com: Best Places to Retire by Level of Education, Health Care, Cost of Living, and Many Other Indicators: http://money.cnn.com/magazines/moneymag/bpretire/2006/top25s/educated.html.
Home Swapping: http://www.homeexchange.com/.
Vacation Rentals: http://www.vacationrentals.com/.
Vacation Rentals by Owners: http://www.vrbo.com/.

REFERENCES

Lapsley, J. N. (2001). "Overcontrol in Retirement Communities." *Pastoral Psychology* 49 (6).
Pulliam Weston, L. "Home Sweet Home: The Hottest Place to Retire." http://articles.moneycentral.msn.com/RetirementandWills/RetireInStyle/HomeSweetHomeTheHottestPlaceToRetire.aspx.
Streib, G. F. (2002). "An Introduction to Retirement Communities." *Research on Aging* 24: 3.

CHAPTER 13

Staying Healthy

Good relationships are enhanced when partners are healthy. Because good health is so important in later life, this chapter discusses preventing or at least significantly delaying some common health problems often associated with aging so that you can enjoy your loved ones and the good things in life for a significantly long period of time. As you will see, there are many things that we can do to keep ourselves healthy. Good health isn't just a crap shoot, but you can add years to your life by a few important steps. They are outlined in the following sections.

TAKING CARE OF YOURSELF: SOME GENERAL ADVICE

In their research on successful aging, Vaillant and Mukamal (2001) believe that we can identify the predictors of longer and healthier lives before the age of 50. Seven health-related behaviors have been identified that lead to longer and healthier lives, indicating that you can have personal control over your physical and emotional health. They are:

- The absence of alcohol abuse and smoking.
- The presence of marital/relationship stability.
- Exercise.
- Normal body mass index indicating appropriate weight for your age and height.

- The ability to cope with stress.
- Involvement in continuing education and intellectual and creative growth.

A number of researchers writing about older adults discuss the concept of successful aging. To give you an example of what is meant by successful aging, Vaillant and Mukamal (2001) identify the following indicators:

- Although elderly people taking three to eight medications a day were seen as chronically ill by their physicians, the people deemed to be aging successfully saw themselves as healthier than their peers.
- Elderly adults who age successfully have the ability to plan ahead and are still intellectually curious and in touch with their creative abilities.
- Successfully aging adults, even those over 95, see life as being meaningful and are able to use humor in their daily lives.
- Aging successfully includes remaining physically active and continuing activities (walking, for example) that were engaged in at an earlier age to remain healthy.
- Older adults who age successfully are more serene and spiritual in their outlook on life than those who age less well.
- Successful aging includes concern for continued friendships; positive interpersonal relationships; satisfaction with spouses, children, and family life; and social responsibility in the form of volunteer work and civic involvement.

In his research on aging, Vaillant (2002) found that the following contributed to successful aging:

- Seeking and maintaining quality relationships.
- Having interest and concern for others.
- Having a sense of humor and the ability to laugh and play well into later life.
- Making new friends as we lose older ones. Vaillant found that quality friendships have a more positive impact on aging well than retirement income.

- Maintaining a desire to learn and to be open to new ideas and new points of view.

- Understanding and accepting our limitations and, when necessary, accepting the help of others.

- Understanding the past and its effect on our lives while living in the present.

- Focusing on the positives and the good people in our lives rather than on negative things that may have happened to us.

Robert and Li (2001) report that despite a usual belief that higher income in retirement positively affects health; research actually suggests a limited relationship between income and health. Rather, there seems to be a relationship between living in an environmentally healthy community with good health care and community concerns about health and one's own health. Lawton (1977) suggests that older adults may experience communities as their primary source of support, recreation, and stimulation, unlike younger adults who find it easier to move about in search of support and recreation. The researchers believe that positive community environments are particularly important to older adults who have health problems that limit their mobility.

Robert and Li (2001) suggest three indicators of healthy communities that directly affect individual health:

- A physical environment with an absence of noise and traffic and with adequate street lighting.

- An absence of crime, the ability to find safe places to walk in, and easy access to shopping.

- A rich service environment that includes simple and safe access to rapid and inexpensive transportation, the availability of senior centers, and easy access to meal sites.

PREVENTING ALZHEIMER'S

One of the most disturbing illnesses associated with aging is Alzheimer's disease (AD). Although the risk factors for developing this disease increase as we age, there is promising new research suggesting that it may be possible to limit that risk.

The symptoms of dementia include loss of memory, extreme mood changes, and communication problems, which include a decline in the ability to talk, write, and read. While AD is the most common disease in which dementia is a symptom, people with dementia may suffer from the effects of strokes and heart problems causing brain damage due to oxygen deprivation. Dementia can also result, to a lesser extent, from the conditions of multiple sclerosis, motor neuron disease, Parkinson's disease, and Huntington's disease.

Brain fitness activities, especially physical activity and aerobic exercise, are believed to protect cognition and benefit memory in midlife (Colcombe and colleagues 2006; Richards and colleagues 2002). Other studies have found that a revolutionary computer-based program can potentially "revitalize the brain" (George 2007), and improvements were found in areas of short-term memory and attention among the participants. Carle (2007) discusses several brain-training games such as "Nana" Technology, Posit Science, Mindfit and MyBrainTrainer.com, in which he describes programs that are "more than just a game" to maintain cognitive strength among older adults. George (2007) states that there is a "life-long ability to adapt, called brain plasticity and the ability to generate new brain cells."

A study published in the *Annals of Neurology* (Scarmeas 2006) suggests that people who eat a "Mediterranean" diet—rich in fruits, vegetables, olive oil, legumes, cereals, and fish—have a lower risk of developing AD. Researchers examined the health and diet of more than 2,000 people over a four-year period. The average age of study participants was 76 and none of the participants had AD at the start of the study. By the end of the study, only 260 participants had been diagnosed with AD. Over the course of the study, researchers evaluated how closely participants followed a published definition of the Mediterranean diet. Participants who stuck most closely to the diet were less likely to develop AD than were participants who didn't follow the diet.

Lunde (2008) believes there is growing evidence suggesting that physical activity may have benefits beyond a healthy heart and body weight. Through the past several years, population studies have suggested that exercise which raises your heart rate for at least 30 minutes several times a week can lower your risk of AD. Physical activity appears to inhibit AD-like brain changes in mice, slowing the development of a key feature of the disease.

In another study, investigators looked at the relationship between physical activity and mental functioning in about 6,000 women aged 65 and older over an eight-year period. They found that the women who were more physically active were less likely to experience a decline in their mental function than inactive women.

Researchers at the University of Chicago conducted another compelling study. The study used mice bred to develop AD-type plaque in their brains. In the study, some mice were allowed to exercise and others were not. The brains in the physically active mice had 50–80 percent less plaque than the brains of the sedentary mice, and the exercising mice produced significantly more of an enzyme in the brain that prevents plaque.

A promising but preliminary study suggests that elderly people who view themselves as self-disciplined, organized achievers may have a lower risk for developing AD than people who are less conscientious (Wilson, Schneider, Arnold, Bienias, and Bennett 2007). According to the researchers, a strong self-directed personality may somehow protect the brain, perhaps by increasing neural connections that can act as a reserve against mental decline. Surprisingly, when the brains of some of the strongly self-directed people in the study were autopsied after their deaths, they were found to have lesions that would meet accepted criteria for AD—even though these people had shown none of the signs of dementia. The authors point out that prior studies have linked social connections and stimulating activities like working puzzles with a lower risk of AD, while people who experience more distress and worry about their lives are at a higher risk.

At the start of the study, none of the participants (997 older Catholic priests, nuns, and monks who participated in the Religious Orders Study) showed signs of dementia. The average age was 75. The subjects were given IQ tests and tests to measure self-direction (conscientiousness) and then were tracked for 12 years. Everyone took tests, including a standard personality test, and then the researchers tracked them for 12 years, with testing done yearly to determine if there were signs of cognitive decline and dementia. Brain autopsies were performed on most of those who died.

Over the 12 years, 176 people developed AD, but those with the highest scores for "conscientiousness" at the start of the study had an 89 percent lower risk of developing AD, compared to people with the lowest scores for that personality trait. The conscientiousness scores were based on how people rated themselves, on a scale of 0–4, on how much they agreed with statements such as: "I work hard to accomplish my goals," "I strive for excellence in everything I do," "I keep my belongings clean and neat," and "I'm pretty good about pacing myself so as to get things done on time."

When the researchers took into account a combination of risk factors, including smoking, inactivity, and limited social connections, they still found that the conscientious people had a 54 percent lower risk of AD compared to people with the lowest scores for conscientiousness.

Researchers at the University of North Dakota have been studying the link between diets that are high in fat and the onset of AD. They found that one cup of coffee a day can neutralize the impact of fat on brain functioning and while the relationship between coffee and AD isn't conclusive, the researchers are optimistic that coffee reduces high levels of iron and cholesterol in the brain that have been associated with AD.

PREVENTING HEART PROBLEMS

The following data on heart attacks comes from the American Heart Association (2008):

- There were 650,000 heart-related deaths in the United States in 2005 (one of every four deaths).
- There were 1,200,000 new and recurrent coronary attacks per year.
- About 38% of people who experience a coronary attack in a given year die from it.
- There are 16 million victims of angina (chest pain due to coronary heart disease), heart attack, and other forms of coronary heart disease who are still living (8,700,000 males and 7,300,000 females).
- From 1994 to 2004 the death rate from coronary heart disease declined 33%.

The following information on preventing heart problems comes from the National Institute for Health and Human Services Heart, Lung and Blood Institute Web site (2009):

- **Diet and Blood Pressure.** Eat a heart-healthy diet and keep your blood pressure less than 120/80.
- **Limit Fat.** Only about 7% of your daily calories should come from saturated fat found in meat and poultry, including dairy products. Fats of all types should be limited to 25 to 35% of your daily calories.

- **Fiber.** You should eat plenty of fiber because it lowers the absorption cholesterol and keeps the heart safe. Fiber might include whole-grain cereal, fruits, kidney beans, lentils, chick peas, black-eyed peas, and lima beans.

- **Fish Oil.** Fish is an important source of omega-3 fatty acids, which may help protect you from blood clots and reduce the risk of heart attacks.

- **Exercise.** Unless your doctor cautions you not to, 30 minutes of moderate-intensity activity on most or all days of the week can be very helpful. You can break that up into 10-minute periods three times a day.

- **Lose Weight.** A body mass index (BMI) of more than 25 is considered overweight. You can use the following link supplied by the National Institute of Health and Human Services to determine your body mass: http://www.nhlbisupport.com/bmi/.

- **Reduce Stress:** Exercise is one of the best ways to reduce stress. If that doesn't work you may want to consider dealing with the source of your stress and making changes. Mental health professionals can be very helpful. Your doctor should also be consulted because some forms of stress have a physical cause. Medications can also help reduce stress, but you should try other options since many anti-anxiety medications can reduce sex drive, cause fatigue, and can become habit-forming and difficult to stop using.

- **Quit Smoking.** Tobacco smoke contains more than 4,800 chemicals. Many of these can damage your heart and blood vessels, making them more vulnerable to narrowing of the arteries (atherosclerosis). Atherosclerosis can ultimately lead to a heart attack.

- **Aspirin.** Aspirin protects the heart by breaking up platelets in the blood. A low dose or baby aspirin (81 mg) has been found to be as effective as a full-strength aspirin of 325 mg. To protect your stomach from getting upset, aspirin is available in a coated (enteric) form. Research has found that considering all types of cardiovascular events, patients who took aspirin were 21% less likely to encounter potentially fatal problems than those who did not.

PREVENTING DIABETES

The American Diabetes Association (2008) reports that 12.2 million, or 23.1 percent of all people 60 and over, have diabetes. The following data on the impact of the disease comes from the American Diabetes Association:

- In 2004, heart disease was noted on 68% of diabetes-related death certificates among people aged 65 years or older.
- In 2004, stroke was noted on 16% of diabetes-related death certificates among people aged 65 years or older.
- Adults with diabetes have heart disease death rates about two to four times higher than adults without diabetes.
- The risk for stroke is two to four times higher among people with diabetes.
- According to death certificate reports, diabetes contributed to a total of 233,619 deaths in 2005, the latest year for which data on contributing causes of death are available.
- Diabetes is the leading cause of new cases of blindness among adults aged 20–74 years. Diabetic retinopathy causes 12,000 to 24,000 new cases of blindness each year.
- Diabetes is the leading cause of kidney failure, accounting for 44% of new cases in 2005.
- About 60–70% of people with diabetes have mild to severe forms of nervous system damage. The results of such damage include impaired sensation or pain in the feet or hands, slowed digestion of food in the stomach, carpal tunnel syndrome, erectile dysfunction, or other nerve problems.
- Severe forms of diabetic nerve disease are a major contributing cause of lower-extremity amputations.

Although there are many reasons for the high rates of diabetes among older adults, including heredity, pancreatic disease, and cardiovascular problems, the primary reason is obesity coupled with inactivity and a diet high in carbohydrates. Like many of us, a friend of mine began putting on weight in his fifties, although he was still an avid tennis player. He was told by doctors he saw about a high blood sugar reading for at least five years before he did anything about it. Six months before he was diagnosed with Type 2 (non-insulin dependent) diabetes, he said that he was about 60 pounds overweight and not very active. His doctor called to say his three-month average blood sugars (called a Hemoglobin A1C test) were high. How high? 7.8, or an average blood sugar of 170–180. Normal is 100 and below.

He said he promised himself that he would lose weight, but that was easier said then done. Five months later he got violently ill and found out that his blood sugars had risen to 260, a seriously high number. He was placed on a well-known diabetes medication called Metformin and also promptly lost 40 pounds. Within two months, his blood sugars were around 100 fasting in the morning. He returned to tennis, began hiking, and started a diet low in carbohydrates (sugar). He'd still like to lose 20 pounds. It's tough, he told me, since weight loss isn't that easy, but he had his scare and it's had a positive impact on his health. He no longer needs diabetes medication. His waist size has dropped from 44" to 38". He plays two hours of singles tennis against much younger opponents and feels healthier than he has in years. He's stopped drinking alcohol, since the thought of it is repugnant to him now. Having gone to a diabetes dietician, he follows her advice and feels content with his diet. It's almost a religious experience, he says, because the discipline has changed his life, including his work habits, and he feels extraordinarily healthy.

Preventing diabetes involves the following:

- Keeping your weight at its suggested level.
- Being active every day for an hour.
- Following a healthy low-fat, low-carbohydrate diet.
- Not smoking and drinking only small amounts of alcohol.
- Keeping stress in check.
- Having your blood sugars checked periodically. You can buy blood sugar monitors cheaply and check your blood sugars in the morning when you wake up and before dinner. If your readings are frequently above 120, see your doctor. It's a sign that something's wrong.
- If your blood pressure is high, your waist is over 40" for men and 34" for women, and your cholesterol is high, then you're at very high risk for heart difficulties.

SUMMARY

This chapter discusses maintaining good health before and after retirement. Special attention was paid to common health problems of older adults including heart problems, adult onset diabetes, and the loss of cognitive functioning related to Alzheimer's and other forms of brain disorders. Special attention was given to recognizing problems as they occur and then seeking out appropriate medical care.

USEFUL WEB SITES

Alzheimer's Association: http://www.alz.org/index.asp.
American Heart Association: http://www.americanheart.org/presenter.jhtml ?identifier=1200000.
Diabetes Information (American Diabetes Association): http://www .diabetes.org/home.jsp.
Senior Health (Medline Plus): http://www.nlm.nih.gov/medlineplus/ seniorshealth.html.
Young at Heart (Government Web site for health tips for older adults): http://www.alz.org/index.asp.

REFERENCES

American Diabetes Association (2008). "Diabetes Statistics." Retrieved November 25, 2009 from: http://www.diabetes.org/diabetes-basics/ diabetes-statistics/.
Carle, A. (2007). "More Than a Game: Brain Training Against Dementia." Feature article in *Nursing Home Magazine*: 22–24.
Colcombe, S., Erickson, K., Scalf, P., Kim, J., Prakash, R., McAuley, E., Elavsky, S., Marquez, D., Hu, L., and Kramer, A. (2006). "Aerobic Exercise Training Increases Brain Volume in Aging Humans." *Journal of Gerontology: Medical Sciences* 61A: 1166–70.
Duke University Medical Center (2008). "Aspirin in Heart Attack Prevention: How Much, How Long?" http://www.dukemednews.org/news/ article.php?id=10217.
George, L. (2007). "The Secret to Not Losing Your Marbles." *Maclean's*: 36–39. Retrieved February 10, 2010 from: http://www.macleans.ca/ homepage/magazine/article.jsp?content=20070409_104109_104109.
"How Is Coronary Artery Disease Treated?" National Institute of Health and Human Services Heart, Lung and Blood Institute. Found on the Internet November 25, 2009 at: http://www.nhlbi.nih.gov/health/dci/ Diseases/Cad/CAD_Treatments.html.
Lawton, M. P. (1977). "The Impact of the Environment on Aging and Behavior." In Birren, J. E., and Schaie, K. W. (eds.), *Handbook of the Psychology of Aging*. New York: Van Nostrand Reinhold: 276–301.
Lunde, A. (March 24, 2008). "Preventing Alzheimer's: Exercise Still Best Bet." http://www.mayoclinic.com/health/alzheimers/MY00002.

Robert, S. A., and Li, L. W. (2001). "Age Variation in the Relationship Between Community, Socioeconomic Status, and Adult Health." *Research on Aging* 23 (2): 233–58.

Scarmeas, N., Stern, Y., Tang, M. X., Mayeux, R., and Luchsinger, J. (April 18, 2006). "Mediterranean Diet and Risk of Alzheimer's Disease." *Annals of Neurology*. http://www.eurekalert.org/pub_releases/2006-04/jws-mdl041106.php/.

Vaillant, G. E. (2002). *Aging Well*. New York: Little, Brown and Company.

Vaillant, G. E., and Mukamal, K. (2001). "Successful Aging." *American Journal of Psychiatry* 158 (6): 839–47.

Wilson, R. S., Schneider, J. A., Arnold, S. E., Bienias, J. L., and Bennett, D. A. (October 20, 2007). "Conscientiousness and the Incidence of Alzheimer Disease and Cognitive Impairment." *Archives of General Psychiatry* 64: 1204, 1212.

CHAPTER 14

Dealing with Later-Life Anxiety and Depression

INTRODUCTION

Among the primary problems that interfere with older adult relationships are emotional difficulties as we age, including anxiety and depression. This chapter discusses why older adults suffer from anxiety and depression, how those problems interfere with life, and what can be done to resolve emotional problems when they begin to intrude on relationships and life happiness.

Large numbers of anxious and depressed older adults often go undiagnosed and untreated because underlying symptoms of anxiety and depression are thought to be physical in nature, and professionals frequently believe that older adults are neither motivated for therapy nor find it an appropriate treatment. This often leaves many older adults trying to cope with serious emotional problems without adequate help. As this chapter will report, the number of older adults dealing with anxiety and depression is considerable and growing as the numbers of older adults increase in America. Health problems, loss of loved ones, financial insecurities, lack of a support group, and a growing sense of isolation and lack of worth are common problems among the elderly that lead to serious symptoms of anxiety and depression, problems that often coexist among many older adults. Several case studies are provided that will hopefully help the reader understand that anxiety and depression are problems that can be effectively treated by mental health professionals.

ANXIETY IN OLDER ADULTS

The prevalence of anxiety disorders has usually been thought to decrease with age, but recent findings suggest that generalized anxiety is actually a more common problem among the elderly than depression. A study reported by Beekman, Bremmer, and Deeg (1998) found anxiety to affect 7.3 percent of an elderly population as compared to 2 percent for depression in the same population. Lang and Stein (2001) estimate that the total number of older Americans suffering from anxiety could be in excess of 10 percent. Since many anxious elderly people do not meet the standard for anxiety found in a number of research studies, the prevalence of anxiety-related problems in the elderly could be as high as 18 percent and constitutes the most common psychiatric symptoms for older adults (Lang and Stein 2001). Typical physical signs of anxiety include chest pains, heart palpitations, night sweats, shortness of breath, essential hypertension, headaches, and generalized pain. Because physicians often fail to diagnose underlying symptoms of anxiety and depression in elderly patients, the emotional components of the symptoms are frequently not dealt with. Definitions and descriptions of anxiety used to diagnosis younger patients often fail to capture the unique stressors that older adults must deal with. Those stressors include the fragile nature of life while attempting to cope with limited finances, failing health, the death of loved ones, concerns about their own mortality, and a sense of uselessness and hopelessness as their roles as adults become dramatically altered due to age and retirement.

Lang and Stein (2001) found that women have higher rates of anxiety across all age groups, and that older adults who have had anxiety problems in the past are more at risk of the problem worsening as they age. Agoraphobia (the fear of leaving one's home) may also be more likely to have later-life onset as a result of physical limitations, disabilities, unsafe neighborhoods, and other factors that make some older adults fearful of leaving home. Because anxiety in older adults may have a physical base or may realistically be connected to concerns about health, Kogan and colleagues (2000) provide some guidelines for older adults and their families to help distinguish physical and emotional reasons for anxiety.

A physical cause of anxiety is more likely if the onset of anxiety comes suddenly, if the symptoms fluctuate in strength and duration, and if fatigue has been present before the symptoms of anxiety were felt.

The authors identify the following medical problems as reasons for symptoms of anxiety: (1) Medical problems that include endocrine, cardiovascular, pulmonary, or neurological disorders; and (2) the impact of certain medications, most notably, stimulants, beta-blockers (used for high blood pressure), certain tranquilizers, and, of course, alcohol. I have included an entire chapter on alcohol and other substances because they are so commonly used by older adults as a way of self-treating anxiety and depression.

An emotional cause of anxiety is more likely if the symptoms have lasted two or more years with little change in severity and if the person has other coexisting emotional symptoms. However, anxiety may cycle on and off, or a lower level of generalized anxiety may be present which causes the older person a great deal of discomfort. Obsessive concerns about financial issues and health are common and realistic worries that trouble older people. The concerns may be situational, or they may be constant but not serious enough to lead to a diagnosis of anxiety; nonetheless, they cause unhappiness and may actually lead to physical problems including high blood pressure, cardiovascular problems, sleep disorders, and an increased use of alcohol and over-the-counter medications to lessen symptoms of anxiety.

UNDERSTANDING THE DIFFERENT TYPES OF ANXIETY IN OLDER ADULTS

The American Psychiatric Association (1994) defines the following anxiety disorders in the adult population:

1. Panic disorders with or without agoraphobia. The chief characteristic of panic disorder is the occurrence of panic attacks coupled with fear of their recurrence. People with agoraphobia are afraid of places or situations in which they might have a panic attack and be unable to leave or find help.
2. Phobias. These include specific phobias and social phobia. A phobia is an intense irrational fear of a specific object or situation that compels the person to avoid it. Some phobias concern activities or objects that involve some risk (for example, flying or driving), but many are focused on harmless animals or other objects. Social phobia involves a fear of being humiliated, judged, or scrutinized; fear of performing certain functions in the presence of others,

such as public speaking, going to social functions and other social events that can result in feelings of loneliness and isolation.

3. Obsessive-compulsive disorder (OCD). This disorder is marked by unwanted, intrusive, persistent thoughts or repetitive behaviors that reflect the person's anxiety or attempts to control it. A compulsion is a repetitive or ritualistic behavior that a person performs to reduce anxiety. Compulsions often develop as a way of controlling or "undoing" obsessive thoughts. An obsession is a repetitive or persistent thought, idea, or impulse that is perceived as inappropriate and distressing.

4. Stress disorders. These include post-traumatic stress disorder (PTSD) and acute stress disorder. Stress disorders are reactions to traumatic events in the patient's life.

5. Generalized anxiety disorder (GAD). GAD is the most commonly diagnosed anxiety disorder and occurs in as many as 7% of healthy older adults. GAD is characterized by difficulty relaxing, constant anticipation of something awful happening, and difficulty controlling this worry or concern. Psychological symptoms may include uncontrollable worry or nervousness, edginess, irritability, and difficulty concentrating. GAD shows itself in physical symptoms including fatigue, low energy, muscle tension, restlessness, and difficulty sleeping.

6. Anxiety disorders due to known physical causes. These include general medical conditions or substance abuse.

PERSONAL STORY: SOCIAL ANXIETY

There are a number of ways of helping older adults with anxiety problems by using family support and understanding, plus medication and counseling. When anxiety problems are severe or interfere with life, it is wise for loved ones to seek professional help. The following story discusses anxiety in a 68-year-old male and his attempts to resolve the problem:

"I'm 68 and I've been anxious in social situations for as long as I can remember. I don't feel anxiety when I do professional presentations or in my work life, but when it comes to meeting people at parties I feel like that famous story of William Faulkner at a party in Hollywood. He was so uncomfortable that he kept backing up toward the balcony of the home where the party was being held until he fell over the balcony and landed in the swimming pool. That's the way I feel at parties. It's agony. I avoid parties or social activities where I don't know people, and even if I *do* know them, I assume people will ignore me or avoid me, which is even worse.

"My brother and sister both feel the same way, so I have to guess that these feelings of anxiety have much to do with our upbringing as Jewish people in a small anti-Semitic town where my immigrant parents moved from Eastern Europe in the 1920s. My parents didn't want us socializing with non-Jewish people, whom they said would never accept us. I think we all felt like outsiders. Even as a kid I didn't think people liked me much and I still feel that way. One of my friends says that maybe I put up a shield that tells people to lay off. It might be true, but whatever I do, the end result is that social events are agony and I feel awful about myself when I go, and just as awful when I decide to avoid them.

"Maybe I'm an anxious person to begin with. I worry a lot, and I always seem to think the worst is going to happen. For several of years in my mid-forties I was on medication for generalized anxiety that was so bad I went into therapy. It didn't help much and neither did the medication. Gradually, as I divorced and eliminated many of my responsibilities, I became a lot less anxious. I sleep well now and I'm productive, but up until my early fifties I guess you could say I was pretty anxious.

"I also notice that I obsess about people and the slights I imagine they've done to me. I feel absolute blinding hatred for anyone who's critical of me. If I play golf and someone says something mean or obnoxious about the way I play, or look, or the clothes I wear, I think about it for weeks. It's all I can do not to wrap my club around their heads. Who knows where this hostility comes from? I don't, and I've been in enough therapy that I should know by now.

"I've concluded that life isn't a box of chocolates and that Forrest Gump was wrong. It's tough, and you have to hang on tight or you'll just fly off into space and never be seen again. I guess I feel that way often, that I'm invisible and when I die, no one will even remember me. I don't know, you work hard, you try your best, you do the things no one else can do, and still you end up feeling unloved and unwanted. It's like a knife in your heart where your feelings live. The anxiety mystifies me. What am I anxious about? I don't know. Maybe magically something will happen and I won't care about other people. Maybe I'll get it right when I'm 70. Two years to go. It can't happen soon enough."—J. G.

DEPRESSION IN OLDER ADULTS

Wallis (2000) believes that older adults express depression through such physical complaints as insomnia, eating disorders, and digestive problems. They may also show signs of lethargy, have less incentive to participate in the activities they enjoyed before they became depressed, and experience symptoms of depression while denying that they are depressed. Mild depressions brought on by situational events usually resolve themselves in time, but moderate depression may interfere with daily life activities and can result in social withdrawal and isolation. Serious depression may result in psychotic-like symptoms including hallucinations and a loss of being in touch with reality (Wallis 2000).

Zalaquett and Stens (2006) believe that depression is often undiagnosed and untreated in older adults, causing "needless suffering for the family and for the individual who could otherwise live a fruitful life" (p. 192). The authors point out that we have sufficient evidence that long-standing depression predicts earlier death while recovery leads to prolonged life. Suicide is a significant risk factor for older adult clients suffering from depression. Depression, according to the authors, may increase the risk of physical illnesses and disability. Unützer and colleagues (2003) report that depression affects between 5 and 10 percent of older adults who visit a primary care provider and is a chronic, recurrent problem affecting many older adults, especially those with poor physical health. The authors note that later-life depression has been associated with substantial "individual suffering, functional impairment, losses in health-related quality of life, poor adherence to medical treatments and increased mortality from suicide and medical illnesses" (p. 505).

Casey (1994) reports a study that found rates of suicide among adults 65 and older almost double that of the general population and that the completion rate for suicide among older adults was 1 in 4 as compared to 1 in 100 for the general population, suggesting that older adults are much more likely to see suicide as a final solution rather than a cry for help. Older adults who commit suicide often suffer from major depression, alcoholism, severe medical problems, and social isolation (Casey 1994). Although adults aged 65 and older comprise only 13 percent of the U.S. population, they accounted for 18 percent of the total number of suicides that occurred in 2000. The highest rate of suicide (19.4 per 1,000) was among people aged 85 and over, a figure that is twice the overall national rate. The second highest rate (17.7 per 100,000) is among adults aged 75 to 84.

While primary care doctors are good at detecting depression in older adults, they aren't as good as trained mental health professionals and psychiatrists in effectively treating depression. For that reason it is wise to seek competent professional help when you or a loved one begin to experience depression that is long-lasting and interferes with your life. Counseling and medication have a very positive impact on older adult depression, and research suggests that older depressed adults benefit from professional help at the same high level as younger depressed people.

In trying to understand why people who have experienced combat in their youth, violent death of loved ones, muggings, and other serious traumas are able to continue on in life without signs of impairment, Kramer (2005) believes that many of us are resilient but as we age, resilience weakens and the experiences we had in earlier times in our lives often catch up with us. Kramer writes:

> I have treated a handful of patients who survived horrors arising from war or political repression. They come to depression years after enduring extreme privation. Typically such a person will say: "I don't understand it. I went through___," and here he will name a shameful event of our time. "I lived through *that* and in those months, I never felt *this*." *This* refers to the relentless bleakness of depression, the self as hollow shell. Beset by great evil, a person can be wise, observant and disillusioned and yet not be depressed. Resilience confers its own measure of insight. (p. 53)

Not surprisingly, Mavandadi and colleagues (2007) found that older adults who lack friends and loved ones in their lives had a high rate of depression. They also found that conflict between friends and loved ones increased levels of depression and that when conflict was resolved, symptoms of depression subsided.

CASE STUDY: HELPING A DEPRESSED OLDER ADULT MALE

The following case study and discussion first appeared in Glicken (2005, pp. 227–31). The author wishes to thank Sage Publications for granting permission to use this material.

"Jake Kissman is a 71-year-old widower whose wife, Leni, passed away a year ago. Jake is emotionally adrift and feels lost without Leni's companionship and guidance. He has a troubled relationship with two adult children who live across the country and has been unable to turn to them for solace and support. Like many older men, Jake has no real support group or close friends. Leni's social circle became his, but after her death, her friends left Jake to fend for himself. Jake is a difficult man who is often critical and insensitive. He tends to say whatever enters his mind at the moment, no matter how hurtful it may be, and then is surprised that people take it so badly. 'It's only words,' he says. 'What harm do words do? It's not like smacking somebody.' Before he retired, Jake was a successful salesman and can be charming and witty, but sooner or later, the disregard for others comes through and he ends up offending people.

"Jake's depression shows itself in fatigue, feelings of hopelessness, irritability, and outbursts of anger. He doesn't believe in doctors and never sees them. 'Look what the *momzers* (bastards) did to poor Leni. A healthy woman in her prime and she needed a surgery like I do. They killed her, those butchers.' Jake has taken to pounding on the walls of his apartment whenever noise from his neighbors upsets him. Complaints from surrounding neighbors have resulted in the threat of an eviction. Jake can't manage a move to another apartment by himself, and someone from his synagogue contacted a professional in the community who agreed to visit Jake at his apartment. Jake is happy that he has company, but angry that someone thought he needed help. 'Tell the bastards to stop making so much noise and I'll be fine. The one next door with the dog, shoot her. The one on the other side who bangs the cabinets, do the same. Why aren't *they* being kicked out?'

"The therapist listens to Jake in a supportive way. He never disagrees with him, offers advice, or contradicts him. Jake is still grieving for his wife and her loss has left him without usable coping skills to deal with the pressures of single life. He's angry and depressed. To find out more about Jake's symptoms, the therapist has gone to the literature on anger, depression, and grief. While he recognizes that Jake is a difficult person in any event, the information he found helped him develop a strategy for working with Jake. The therapist has decided to use a strengths approach (Weick et al. 1989; Saleebey 1992; Glicken 2004) with Jake. The strengths approach focuses on what clients have done well in their lives and uses those strengths in areas of life that are more problematic. The approach comes from studies on resilience, self-healing, and successful work with abused and traumatized children and adults.

"Jake has many positive attributes that most people have ignored. He was a warm and caring companion to Leni during her illness. He is secretly very generous and gives what he has to various charities without wanting people to know where his gifts come from. He helps his children financially and has done a number of acts of kindness for neighbors and friends, but in ways that always make the recipients feel ambivalent about his help. Jake is a difficult and complex man, and no one has taken the time to try and understand him. The therapist takes a good deal of time and listens closely.

"Jake feels that he's been a failure at life. He feels unloved and unappreciated. He thinks the possibility of an eviction is a good example of how people 'do him in' when he is least able to cope with stress. So the therapist listens and never disagrees with Jake. Gradually, Jake has begun discussing his life and the sadness he feels without his wife, who was his ballast and mate. Using a strengths approach, the therapist always focuses on what Jake does well and his generosity, while Jake uses their time to beat himself up with self-deprecating statements. The therapist listens, smiles, points out Jake's excellent qualities, and waits for Jake to start internalizing what the therapist has said about him. Gradually, it begins to work. Jake tells the therapist to go help someone who needs it when Jake's anger at the therapist becomes overwhelming. Jake immediately apologizes. 'Here you're helping me and I criticize. Why do I do that?' he asks the therapist. There are many moments when Jake corrects himself or seems to fight an impulse to say something mean-spirited or hurtful to the therapist, who tells him, 'Jake, you catch more flies with honey than you do with vinegar.' To which Jake replies, 'So who needs to catch flies, for crying out loud? Oh, I'm sorry. Yeah, I see what you mean. It's not about flies, it's about getting along with people.'

"Gradually, Jake has put aside his anger and has begun talking to people in the charming and pleasant manner he is so capable of. The neighbors who complained about him now see him as a 'doll.' Jake's depression is beginning to lift and he's begun dating again, although he says he can never love anyone like his wife. 'But a man gets lonely. So what are you supposed to do, sit home and watch soap operas all day? Not me.' The therapist continues to see Jake and they often sit and quietly talk about Jake's life. Jake told him, 'I was a big deal once. I could sell an Eskimo an air conditioner in winter. I could charm the socks off people. But my big mouth, it always got in the way. I always said something that made people mad. Maybe it's because my dad was so mean to all of us, I got this chip on my shoulder. Leni was wonderful.

She could put up with me and make me laugh. When she died, I was left with my big mouth and a lot of disappointments. You want to have friends, you want your kids to love you. I got neither, but I'm not such an *alte cocker* (old fart) that I don't learn. And I've learned a lot from you. I've learned you can teach an old dog new tricks, and that's something. So I thank you and I apologize for some of the things I said. It's hard to get rid of the chip on the shoulder and sometimes it tips you over, that big chip, and it makes you fall down. You're a good person. I wish you well in life.' "

SUMMARY

This chapter on older adults experiencing anxiety and depression points out the frequency and severity of both problems in older adults and the high rate of completion of suicide, particularly in aging men. The chapter also notes the importance of seeking help from trained mental health professionals and that counseling and medication can help older adults at the same levels as younger adults. A case study and a story show how older adults are affected by anxiety and depression and how counseling can often be helpful.

REFERENCES

DEPRESSION

American Psychiatric Association (1994). *Diagnostic and Statistical Manual of Mental Disorders* (4th ed.). Washington, D.C.: APA.

Axelson, J. A. (1985). *Counseling and Development in a Multicultural Society.* Monterey, CA: Brooks/Cole.

Blazer, D. G. (1993). *Depression in Late Life* (2nd ed.). St. Louis, MO: Mosby.

Blazer, D. G., Hughes, D. C., and George, L. K. (1987). "The Epidemiology of Depression in an Elderly Community Population." *Journal of the American Geriatric Society* 27: 281–87.

Casey, D. A. (1994). "Depression in the Elderly." *Southern Medical Journal,* 87 (5): 559–64.

Centers for Disease Control and Prevention, National Center for Injury Prevention and Control (2005). Web-based Injury Statistics Query and Reporting System (WISQARS). Accessed January 31, 2007. Available from URL: www.cdc.gov/ncipc/wisqars.

Charbonneau, A., Rosen, A. K., Ash, A. S., Owen, R. R., Kader, B., Spiro III, A., et al. (2003). "Measuring the Quality of Depression Care in a Large Integrated Health System." *Med Care* 41: 669–80.

Gallagher-Thompson, D., Hanley-Peterson, P., and Thompson, L. W. (1990). "Maintenance of Gains Versus Relapse Following Brief Psychotherapy for Depression." *Journal of Consulting and Clinical Psychology* 58: 371–74.

Glicken, M. D. (2003). *A Simple Guide to Social Research*. Boston, MA: Allyn and Bacon/Longman.

———— (2004). *The Strengths Perspective in Social Work Practice: A Positive Approach for the Helping Professions*. Boston, MA: Allyn and Bacon/Longman.

Hepner, K. A., Rowe, M., Rost, K., Hickey, S. C., Sherbourne, C. D., Ford, D. E., Meredith, L. S., and Rubenstein, L. V. (September 2007). "The Effect of Adherence to Practice Guidelines on Depression Outcomes." *Annals of Internal Medicine* 147 (5): 320–29.

Huffman, G. B. (1999). "Preventing Recurrence of Depression in the Elderly." *American Family Physician* 59 (9): 2589–91.

Kennedy, G. J., and Tannenbaum, S. (2000). "Psychotherapy with Older Adults." *American Journal of Psychotherapy* 54 (3): 386–407.

Kramer, P. D. (April 17, 2005). "There's Nothing Deep about Depression." *New York Times Magazine*: 50–53.

Lawton, M. P. (1977). "The Impact of the Environment on Aging and Behavior." In Birren, J. E., and Schaie, K. W. (eds.), *Handbook of the Psychology of Aging*. New York: Van Nostrand Reinhold: 276–301.

Lawton, M. P., and Nahemow, L. (1973). "Ecology and the Aging Process." In Eisdorfer, C., and Lawton, M. P. (eds.), *The Psychology of Adult Development and Aging*. Washington, D.C.: American Psychological Association: 619–74.

Lebowitz, B. D., Pearson, J. D., Schneider, L. S., Reynolds III, C. F., Alexopoulos, G. S., Bruce, M. L., Conwell, Y., Katz, I. R., Meyers, B. S., Morrison, M. F., Mossey, J., Niederehe, G., and Parmelee, P. (1997). "Diagnosis and Treatment of Depression in Late Life: Consensus Statement Update." *Journal of the American Medical Association* 278 (14): 1186–90.

Lenze, E. J., Dew, M. A., Mazumdar, S., Begley, A. E., et al. (2002). "Combined Pharmacotherapy and Psychotherapy as Maintenance Treatment for Late-Life Depression: Effects on Social Adjustment." *American Journal of Psychiatry* 159 (3): 466–68.

Mavandadi, I., Sorkin, D. H., Rook, K. S., and Newsom, J. T. (October 2007). "Pain, Positive and Negative Social Exchanges, and Depressive Symptomatology in Later Life." *Journal of Aging and Health* 19 (5): 813–30.

Mills, T. L., and Henretta, J. C. (2001). "Racial, Ethnic, and Socio-demographic Differences in the Level of Psychosocial Distress among Older Americans." *Research on Aging* 23 (2): 131–52.

Myers, J. E., and Harper, M. C. (Spring 2004). "Evidence-based Effective Practices with Older Adults." *Journal of Counseling & Development* 82: 207–18.

NIH Consensus Panel on Diagnosis and Treatment of Depression in Late Life (1992). "Diagnosis and Treatment of Depression in Late Life." *Journal of the American Medical Association* 268: 1018–24.

Pinquart, M., and Sörensen, S. (2001). "How Effective Are Psychotherapeutic and Other Psychosocial Interventions with Older Adults? A Meta-analysis." *Journal of Mental Health & Aging* 7: 207–43.

Plopper, M. (1990). "Evaluation and Treatment of Depression." In Kemp, B., Brummel-Smith, K., and Ramsdell, J. W. (eds.), *Geriatric Rehabilitation*. Boston: College-Hill: 253–64.

Robert, S. A., and Li, L. W. (2001). "Age Variation in the Relationship Between Community Socioeconomic Status and Adult Health." *Research on Aging* 23 (2): 233–58.

Roth, A. D., and Fonagy, E. (1996). *What Works with Whom? A Critical Review of Psychotherapy Research*. New York: Guilford Press.

Rush, A. J., and Giles, D. E. (1982). *Cognitive Therapy: Theory and Research in Short Term Psychotherapies for Depression*. New York: Guilford Press: 143–81.

Saleebey, D. (1992). *The Strengths Perspective in Social Work Practice*. White Plains, NY: Longman.

Thompson, L. W., Gallager, D., and Breckenridge, J. S. (1987). "Comparative Effectiveness of Psychotherapies for Depressed Elders." *Journal of Consulting and Clinical Psychology* 55: 385–90.

Tyler, K. A., and Hoyt, D. R. (2000). "The Effects of an Acute Stressor on Depressive Symptoms among Older Adults." *Research on Aging* 22 (2): 143–64.

Unützer, J., Katon, W., Callahan, C. M., Williams, J. W., Hunkeler, E., Harpole, L., Hoffing, M., Della Penna, R. D., Noel, P. H., Lin, E. H. B., Vaillant, G. E., and Mukamal, K. (2001). "Successful Aging." *American Journal of Psychiatry* 158 (6): 839–47.

Wallis, M. A. (2000). "Looking at Depression Through Bifocal Lenses." *Nursing* 30 (9): 58–62.

Weick, A., Rapp, C., Sullivan, W. P., and Kisthardt, W. (1989). "A Strengths Perspective for Social Work Practice." *Social Work* 34: 350–54.

Zalaquett, C. P., and Stens, A. N. (Spring 2006). "Psychosocial Treatments for Major Depression and Dysthymia in Older Adults: A Review of the Research Literature." *Journal of Counseling & Development* 84: 192–201.

Anxiety

Aarts, P., and Op den Velde, W. (1996). "Prior Traumatization and the Process of Aging." In van der Kolk, B. A., McFarlane, A. C., and Weisath, L. (eds.), *Traumatic Stress: The Effects of Overwhelming Experience on Mind, Body and Society.* New York: Guilford Press: 359–77.

Beck, J. G., and Stanley, M. A. (1997). "Anxiety Disorders in the Elderly: The Emerging Role of Behavior Therapy." *Behavior Therapy* 28: 83–100.

Beekman, A. T., Bremmer, M. A., Deeg, D. J. H., et al. (1998). "Anxiety Disorders in Later Life: A Report from the Longitudinal Aging Study Amsterdam." *International Journal of Geriatric Psychiatry* 12 (10): 717–26.

Kogan, J. N., Edelstein, B. A., and McKee, D. R. (2000). "Assessment of Anxiety in Older Adults: Current Status." *Journal of Anxiety Disorders* 14 (2): 109–32.

Lang, A. J., and Stein, M. B. (2001). "Anxiety Disorders." *Geriatrics* 56 (5): 24–30.

McFarlane, A. C., and Yehuda, R. (1996). "Resilience, Vulnerability, and the Course of Post-traumatic Reactions." In van der Kolk, B. A., McFarlane, A. C., and Weisath, L. (eds.), *Traumatic Stress: The Effects of Overwhelming Experience on Mind, Body, and Society.* New York: Guilford Press: 155–81.

Pingitore, D., and Sansone, R. A. (October 15, 1998). "Using DSM-IV Primary Care Version: A Guide to Psychiatric Diagnosis in Primary Care." *American Family Physician* 58 (6).

Smith, S. S., Sherrill, K. A., and Celenda, C. C. (1995). "Anxious Elders Deserve Careful Diagnosing and the Most Appropriate Interventions." *Brown University Long-Term Care Letter* 7 (10): 5–7.

Stanley, M. A., and Novy, D. M. (2000). "Cognitive-Behavior Therapy for Generalized Anxiety in Late Life: An Evaluative Overview." *Journal of Anxiety Disorders* 14 (2): 191–207.

Surgeon General's Report: Older Adults and Mental Health (Anxiety Disorders, Chapter 5) (1999). http://www.surgeongeneral.gov/library/mentalhealth/chapter5/sec5.html#anxiety.

Wagner, K. D., and Lorion, R. P. (1984). "Correlates of Death Anxiety in Elderly Persons." *Journal of Clinical Psychology* 40: 1235–41.

CHAPTER 15

Older Adults Who Abuse Alcohol and Drugs

INTRODUCTION

I've included a chapter on substance abuse because it's one of the most common problems facing older adults and one that often wrecks relationships and destroys older adult happiness. Substance abuse can take the form of alcohol abuse, legal prescription drug abuse, and illegal drug usage. Often these problems come earlier in life, but in some cases they begin to develop after retirement or in later life. Because of health problems that result from substance abuse, it is very important to recognize actual or potential problems with substance abuse and do something definite about it. This chapter describes the conditions under which substance abuse is considered a health problem, the treatment used with moderate substance abuse problems in older adults, and a case example of an older adult woman abusing substances after moving to a retirement community.

THE PREVALENCE OF SUBSTANCE ABUSE IN OLDER ADULTS

Because older adults sometimes experience loneliness and feelings of isolation, alcohol and prescription drug abuse among adults 60 and older is one of the fastest-growing health problems facing the country. Blow (2007) believes that "even as the number of older adults suffering from these disorders climbs, the situation remains underestimated, under-identified, under-diagnosed, and under-treated" (p. 1).

Blow reports that substance abuse often has a serious impact on the health of older adults and writes:

> The reality is that misuse and abuse of alcohol and other drugs take a greater toll on affected older adults than on younger adults. In addition to the psychosocial issues that are unique to older adults, aging also ushers in biomedical changes that influence the effects that alcohol and drugs have on the body. Alcohol abuse, for example, may accelerate the normal decline in physiological functioning that occurs with age. In addition, alcohol may elevate older adults' already high risk for injury, illness, and socioeconomic decline. (Blow 2007, p. 2)

There are two widely held myths regarding alcohol use among older adults: (1) that it is an infrequent problem; and (2) that when older adults have drinking problems treatment success is limited. In fact, according to the government, "alcohol abuse among older adults is one of the fastest-growing health problems facing this country (Substance Abuse and Mental Health Services Administration [SAMHSA] 1998) and even a one-time brief encounter of 15 min or less can reduce nondependent problem drinking by more than 20% (SAMHSA)" (p. 454).

According to the National Institute for Alcohol Abuse and Alcoholism (NIAAA 1997), roughly 49 percent of all adults aged 60 years and older drink alcohol. Among those aged 60–64 responding to the national survey on drug use and health sponsored by SAMHSA (2004), 50 percent used alcohol in the past month, and 35 percent of individuals aged 65 or older used alcohol in the past month. 6.9 percent of adults aged 65 or older reported binge drinking and 1.8 percent reported heavy drinking. Binge drinking is defined as five or more drinks on the same occasion on at least one day in the past month. Heavy drinking is defined as five or more drinks on the same occasion on each of five or more days in the past 30 days. Adams, Barry, and Fleming (1996) report that among community-dwelling, non-institutionalized older adults, 2–15 percent have been shown to exhibit symptoms consistent with alcoholism.

Although the data on older adult alcohol abuse suggest a growing problem, it's difficult to pinpoint alcohol abuse in older adults. Even though a third of all heavy drinkers begin their patterns of alcohol abuse after age 60 (Barrick and Connors 2002), many symptoms of problem drinking "mimic" physical problems common to this age group, including depression and dementia. Because of stereotypes of older adults by health care professionals, doctors are often unlikely to screen for alcohol problems, particularly in women and older adults who are well educated or affluent. Because alcohol abuse is still considered a morally offensive problem, older adults with substance abuse problems may feel "ashamed" to discuss the problem with their physicians. And because of stereotypes that older adults want to be left alone or have few opportunities for happiness, some health and mental health professionals believe that drinking is one of the few pleasures left to older men and women.

There are a number of serious health consequences of older adult problem drinking. Oslin (2004) reports that even small to moderate amounts of alcohol can increase the risk of hypertension, sleep problems, and malnutrition. The risk of losing one's balance and falling increases with alcohol consumption and significantly increases when 14 or more drinks are consumed per week (Mukamal, Mittleman, Longstreth, Newman, Fried, and Siscovick 2004). Older adults are vulnerable to the negative effects of alcohol because they take more medications than younger people and are therefore at risk for drug or alcohol interactions. Because of slower metabolic and clearance mechanisms, older adults are also more likely to experience adverse drug and alcohol interactions. Slower metabolic and clearance mechanisms delay the body's ability to rid itself of alcohol in the blood stream. Onder and colleagues (2002) studied alcohol consumption among a population of older adults 65–80 years of age and found that even moderate consumption of alcohol increased the risk of an adverse drug reaction by 24 percent.

RELATED MEDICAL PROBLEMS

Stewart and Richards (2000) conclude that a number of older adult medical problems may have their origins in heavy alcohol and drug use. Head injuries and spinal separations as a result of accidents may have been caused by substance abuse. Because heavy drinkers often fail to eat, they may have nutritional deficiencies, which result in psychotic-like symptoms including abnormal eye movements, disorganization, and forgetfulness. Stomach disorders, liver damage, and severe heartburn may have their origins in heavy drinking because alcohol destroys the stomach's mucosal lining. Fifteen percent of all heavy drinkers develop cirrhosis of the liver and many develop pancreatitis. Weight loss, pneumonia, muscle loss because of malnutrition, and oral cancer have all been associated with heavy drinking. Stewart and colleagues (2000) indicate that substance abusers are poor candidates for surgery. Anesthesia and pain medication can delay alcohol withdrawal for up to five days postoperatively. "Withdrawal symptoms can cause agitation and uncooperativeness and can mask signs and symptoms of other postoperative complications. Patients who abuse alcohol are at a higher risk for postoperative complications such as excessive bleeding, infection, heart failure, and pneumonia" (Stewart and colleagues 2000, p. 58).

HOW TO DETERMINE IF YOU OR A LOVED ONE HAS A SUBSTANCE ABUSE PROBLEM

The manual used to determine whether people have emotional problems called the DSM-IV (APA 1994) uses the following indicators to determine whether substance use is abusive. The first indicator is an overuse of substances causing impairment or distress within a 12-month period as determined by one of the following:

- Frequent use of substances that interfere with functioning and the fulfillment of responsibilities at home, work, school, etc.
- Use of substances that impair functioning in dangerous situations such as driving or the use of machines.
- Use of substances that may lead to arrest for unlawful behaviors.
- Substance use that seriously interferes with relationships, marriage, childrearing, and other interpersonal responsibilities (APA 1994, p. 182).
- Substance abuse may also lead to slurred speech, lack of coordination, unsteady gait, memory loss, fatigue and depression, feelings of euphoria, and lack of social inhibitions (APA 1994, p. 197).

SHORT TESTS

Miller (2001) reports that two simple questions asked of substance abusers have an 80 percent chance of diagnosing substance abuse: "In the past year, have you ever drunk or used drugs more than you meant to?" and "Have you felt you wanted or needed to cut down on your drinking or drug abuse in the past year?" Miller reports that this simple approach has been found to be an effective diagnostic tool in three controlled studies using random samples and laboratory tests for alcohol and drugs in the bloodstream following interviews.

Stewart and colleagues (2000) and Bisson and colleagues (1999) suggest that four questions from the CAGE questionnaire are predictive of alcohol abuse. CAGE is an acronym for Cut, Annoyed, Guilty, and Eye-Opener (see the questions below). Since many people deny their alcoholism, asking questions in an open, direct and nonjudgmental way may elicit the best results. The four questions are:

1. **Cut.** Have you ever felt you should cut down on your drinking?
2. **Annoyed.** Have people annoyed you by criticizing your drinking?
3. **Guilty.** Have you ever felt guilty about your drinking?
4. **Eye-Opener.** Have you ever had a drink first thing in the morning (eye-opener) to steady your nerves or get rid of a hangover? (Bisson, Nadeau, and Demers 1999, p. 717)

Stewart and colleagues (2000) write, "A patient who answers yes to two or more of these questions probably abuses alcohol; a patient who answers yes to one question should be screened further" (p. 56).

Should you or a friend or loved one ever be stopped by a police officer and asked to take a test to measure alcohol in the bloodstream, Stewart and colleagues (2000, p. 59) provide the following blood alcohol levels as measures of the impact of alcohol:

- 0.05% (equivalent to one or two drinks in an average-sized person)—impaired judgment, reduced alertness, loss of inhibitions, euphoria.
- 0.10%—slower reaction times, decreased caution in risk-taking behavior, impaired fine-motor control. Legal evidence of intoxication in most states starts at 0.10%.
- 0.15%—significant and consistent losses in reaction times.
- 0.20%—function of entire motor area of brain measurably depressed, causing staggering. The individual may be easily angered or emotional.
- 0.25%—severe sensory and motor impairment.
- 0.30%—confusion, stupor.
- 0.35%—surgical anesthesia.

- 0.40%—respiratory depression, lethal in about half of the population.
- 0.50%—death from respiratory depression (p. 59).

UNDERSTANDING THE TREATMENTS FOR SUBSTANCE ABUSE

SHORT-TERM TREATMENT

Herman (2000) believes that individual counseling can be helpful in treating substance abusers and suggests five situations in which therapy would be indicated:

- As an appropriate introduction to treatment.
- As a way of helping mildly or moderately dependent drug abusers.
- When there are clear signs of emotional problems such as severe depression, since these problems will interfere with the substance abuse treatment.
- When people progressing in 12-step programs begin to experience emerging feelings of guilt, shame, and grief.
- When a person's disturbed interpersonal functioning continues after a long period of sustained abstinence and therapy might help prevent a relapse.

One of the most frequently discussed treatment approaches is brief counseling. Bien and colleagues (1993) reviewed 32 studies of brief interventions with alcohol abusers and found that, on average, brief counseling reduced alcohol use by 30 percent. However, in a study of brief intervention with alcohol abusers, Chang and colleagues (1999) found that both the treatment and control groups significantly reduced their alcohol use. The difference between the two groups in the reduction of their alcohol abuse was minimal. In a study of 175 Mexican-Americans who were abusing alcohol, Burge and colleagues (1997) report that treated and untreated groups improved significantly over time, raising questions about the effectiveness of treatment versus recovery without professional help. In an evaluation of a larger report by *Consumer Reports* on the effectiveness of psychotherapy, Seligman (1995) notes that, "Alcoholics Anonymous (AA) did especially well . . . significantly bettering mental health professionals [in the treatment of alcohol and drug-related problems]" (p. 10).

Bien and colleagues (1993) found that two or three 10–15 minute counseling sessions are often as effective as more extensive interventions with older alcohol abusers. The sessions include motivation-for-change strategies, education, assessment of the severity of the problem, direct feedback, contracting and goal-setting, behavioral modification techniques, and the use of written materials such as self-help manuals. Brief interventions have been shown to be effective in reducing alcohol consumption, binge drinking, and the frequency of excessive drinking in problem drinkers, according to Fleming and colleagues (1997). Completion rates using brief interventions are better for older people than for mixed-age programs (Atkinson 1995), and late-onset alcoholics are more likely to complete treatment and have somewhat better outcomes using brief interventions (Liberto and Oslin 1995).

Some additional aspects of brief interventions suggested by Menninger (2002) include drinking agreements in the form of agreed-upon drinking limits that are signed by the patient and the practitioner, ongoing follow-up and support, and appropriate timing of the intervention with the patient's readiness to change. Completion rates for elder-specific alcohol treatment programs are modestly better than for mixed-age programs (Atkinson 1995). Late-onset alcoholics are also more likely to complete treatment and have somewhat better outcomes (Liberto and Oslin 1995). Alcoholics Anonymous may be helpful, particularly AA groups that are specifically oriented toward the elderly.

Babor and Higgins-Biddle (2000) discuss the use of brief interventions with people involved in "risky drinking" who are not as yet classified as alcohol-dependent. Brief interventions are usually limited to three to five sessions of counseling and education. The intent of brief interventions is to prevent the onset of more serious alcohol-related problems. According to Babor and colleagues (2000), "[m]ost programs are instructional and motivational, designed to address the specific behavior of drinking with information, feedback, health education, skill-building, and practical advice, rather than with psychotherapy or other specialized treatment techniques" (p. 676). Higgins-Biddle and colleagues (1997) analyzed 14 random studies of brief interventions that included more than 20,000 risky drinkers. They report a net reduction in drinking of 21 percent for males and 8 percent for females.

Fleming and Manwell (1998) report that people with alcohol-related problems often receive counseling from primary-care physicians or nursing staff in five or fewer standard office visits. The counseling consists of accurate information about the negative impact of alcohol use as well as practical advice regarding ways of reducing alcohol dependence and the availability of community resources. Gentilello and collleagues (1995) report that 25–40 percent of the trauma patients seen in emergency rooms may be alcohol-dependent. The authors found that a single motivational interview, at or near the time of discharge, reduced drinking levels and readmission for trauma during six months of follow-up.

RECOVERY WITHOUT COUNSELING

Granfield and Cloud (1996) estimate that as many as 90 percent of all problem drinkers never enter treatment and that many end their abuse of alcohol without any form of treatment (Hingson, Scotch, Day, and Culbert 1980; Roizen, Calahan, Lambert, Wiebel, and Shanks 1978; Stall and Biernacki 1989). Sobell, Sobell, Toneatto, and Leo (1993) report that 82 percent of the alcoholics they studied who terminated their addiction did so by using natural recovery methods that excluded the use of professional treatment. As an example of the use of natural recovery techniques, Granfield and Cloud (1996) report that most ex-smokers discontinued their tobacco use without treatment (Peele 1989), while many addicted substance abusers "mature-out" of a variety of addictions including heavy drinking and narcotic use (Snow 1973; Winick 1962). Biernacki (1986) reports that people who use natural methods to end their drug addictions utilize a range of strategies, including discontinuing their relationships with drug users, avoiding drug-using environments (Stall and Biernacki 1986), having new goals and interest in their lives (Peele 1989), and using friends and family to provide a support network (Biernacki 1986). Trice and Roman (1970) indicate that self-help groups with substance-abusing clients are particularly helpful because they develop and continue a support network that assists clients in maintaining abstinence and other changed behaviors.

Granfield and Cloud (1996) studied middle-class alcoholics who used natural recovery alone, without professional help or the use of self-help groups. Many of the participants in their study felt that some self-help groups were overly religious, while others believed in alcoholism as a disease that suggested a lifetime struggle. The subjects in the study believed that some self-help groups encouraged dependence on the group and that associating with other alcoholics would probably complicate recovery. In summarizing their findings, Granfield et al. (1996) report that:

> Many [research subjects] expressed strong opposition to the suggestion that they were powerless over their addictions. Such an ideology, they explained, not only was counterproductive but was also extremely demeaning. These respondents saw themselves as efficacious [competent] people who often prided themselves on their past accomplishments. They viewed themselves as being individualists and strong-willed. One respondent, for instance, explained that "such programs encourage powerlessness" and that she would rather "trust her own instincts than the instincts of others." (Granfield et al. 1996, p. 51)

Waldorf and colleagues (1991) found that many addicted people with jobs, strong family ties, and other close emotional supports were able to "walk away" from their very heavy use of cocaine. Granfield and colleagues (1996) note that many of the respondents in their study had a great deal to lose if they continued their substance abuse and that their sample consisted of people with stable lives, good jobs, supportive families and friends, college educations, and other social supports that gave them motivation to "alter" their drug-using behaviors.

SELF-HELP GROUPS

Humphreys (1998) studied the effectiveness of self-help groups with substance abusers by comparing two groups: one receiving inpatient care for substance abuse, and the other attending self-help groups for substance abuse. At the conclusion of the study, the average participant assigned to a self-help group (AA) had used $8,840 in alcohol-related health care resources as compared to $10,040 for the inpatient treatment participants. In a follow-up study, Humphreys (1998) compared outpatient services to self-help groups for the treatment of substance abuse. The clients in the self-help group had decreased alcohol consumption by 70 percent over three years and consumed 45 percent fewer health care services (about $1,800 less per person).

A RETIRED SINGLE WOMAN CONFRONTS
HER ALCOHOLISM

Wanda Anderson is a 69-year-old single woman who lives in an upscale retirement community in Arizona. Wanda was a successful real estate agent in St. Louis for many years and decided to sell her home at the height of the real estate boom and buy a nice but much less expensive home in a retirement community and invest the profit for retirement income. Wanda moved to her new home in January and was ecstatic to find 70-degree weather and many activities that she could not do in St. Louis during the winter. However, her first summer in Arizona was a shock, with temperatures hovering in the 100–115-degree range for almost six months without stop. During the hot months, Wanda found that many people left for cooler climates and that her fantasy of many close friends to accompany her on "adventures" evaporated. She was alone and there were few people with whom she could socialize. The community had a bar with a happy hour where cheap drinks and food were available, and Wanda began going every afternoon around 4:00 p.m. and staying increasingly later.

Wanda said that she had never been much of a drinker, but after going to happy hour almost every day for a year, she found that thinking about having a drink gave her great joy. She couldn't wait until 4:00 p.m. to begin. The bar was only a short distance from her home and she either walked or drove her electric golf cart. One night, driving home from the bar in her cart about 11:00 p.m. when most people were asleep, Wanda missed a turn and her cart went down a steep embankment. She and a friend were to go walking at 6:00 a.m. the next morning before the summer heat became unbearable. Not finding Wanda at home, the friend contacted security and, after a long search, they found Wanda unconscious at the bottom of the embankment with the cart lying partially on top of her.

Wanda was rushed to the hospital and, thankfully, her injuries were limited to a broken arm and a number of cuts and bruises. More serious was the fact that her blood pressure and blood sugars were extremely high. Wondering about the possibility of alcohol abuse, the attending physician checked her alcohol level and, even after many hours without alcohol, found it high. He also found evidence of the onset of liver damage and possible heart problems.

When Wanda was awake, the doctor and a social worker interviewed her about her accident and her alcohol consumption. At first she was very defensive, but after a few minutes of avoiding their questions she admitted that she drank 10–15 drinks, usually martinis, every day at the bar and had even begun having a few drinks before happy hour. A social worker and nurse met with Wanda three additional times over the course of a three-day stay in the hospital. They gave her information about the health impact of drinking and performed a screening test to determine Wanda's level of abusive drinking. They concluded that she was at very high risk of becoming an alcoholic, since her drinking impaired her judgment and was thought to be responsible for high blood pressure and high blood sugar readings consistent with adult-onset diabetes.

A history taken by the social worker revealed that Wanda was painfully lonely and that the drinking seemed to be a response to early retirement without a plan for what she would do with herself after a lifetime of hard, successful work. The history also revealed that Wanda had come from a family of alcoholics and had vowed to keep her drinking limited, but now realized she was romanticizing alcohol the same way many members of her family had. Wanda had her driver's license revoked, and her ability to drive her golf cart in the retirement community grounds was curtailed to daylight hours and then only if someone was with her. She was told by the retirement community CEO that the bylaws of the community required her to go for counseling, and that she had to maintain sobriety for six months before she could have full use of her cart privileges. She was also banned from any of the bars in the retirement community.

Wanda met with her substance abuse counselor and for the first few sessions was very angry and could only talk about the "hoity-toity" CEO and who did he think he was? She'd seen lots of men like him and she would just like to tell him a thing or two. But in the third session, Wanda broke down and cried, telling the counselor she made a mistake retiring and leaving her support network in St. Louis. Little did she know, she told the counselor, that she had an aversion to "old people" and hated it here in the community. She thought she'd meet a man but most of the men were either "jerks, or the same Casanovas she'd been meeting most of her life," or they were too old and sick to be any fun. She'd spent her first 18 years taking care of "drunks" and she never wanted to take care of anyone again. Still, she was lonely, and loneliness, she admitted, was everything it was cracked up to be.

The first item on the agenda was to focus on resolving the alcohol problem and the issues that seemed to bring about the later-life drinking problem. After some discussion, Wanda pointed out that she didn't like the words "alcoholic" or "drunk," since they were words used to describe members of her family. She did agree that she was drinking too much and that the drinking had health and mental health implications. The social worker asked that Wanda do what she had done so often in her lifetime, and that was to take control of her problem by assertively looking for more information that she could use in counseling. Wanda agreed and the worker gave her a list of articles on the Internet she might read for the next session and encouraged Wanda do her own reading about later-life drinking problems, loneliness, and early retirement.

From the reading of articles suggested by the social worker, they agreed that Wanda had a number of problems that should be dealt with, including feelings of loneliness, lack of work to keep her occupied, little ability to handle leisure time, and alcohol abuse. Wanda brought up the issue of understanding the impact her alcoholic family had on her current situation.

After months of treatment, during which Wanda would often avoid answering questions directly or would go off on tangents, she began to talk about her feelings and admitted that she has continued drinking heavily. She also drives, although her license has been suspended. She feels strong when she drinks, and loves the peaceful feeling that comes over her as she gets drunk. Like her parents, she romanticizes her drinking and can hardly wait to have her first drink of the day. Sometimes she drinks when she wakes up and often drinks rather than eating. She is aware that this cycle of drinking to feel better about herself can only lead to serious life problems, but she doesn't think she's capable of stopping. A number of women in the community are secret drinkers, she tells the counselor, and like many of them, drinking is one of the few pleasures they have. Life has stopped having meaning and, faced with many years of living alone and doing nothing, she finds solace in alcohol.

Her counselor has seen the same pattern in older adult alcoholics and has allowed for the fact that the problem will take much longer to resolve because Wanda lacks a support group. The therapist thought that an older adult support group of problem drinkers at the retirement community would help Wanda, but learned from Wanda that all the members have continued drinking and have even formed a club of sorts to drink together.

During one session several months into treatment, the counselor admitted to Wanda that the treatment wasn't helping Wanda with her drinking. While Wanda read articles and came prepared to discuss them, it was an intellectual exercise and it wasn't helping Wanda change her behavior. Wanda pleaded with the counselor not to give up on her. She was the only person in Wanda's life with whom Wanda could talk. She didn't know what she would do if the counselor gave up on her and had openly considered suicide as an option.

The session was electric, as Wanda spoke of her early life and her codependency and how it had made relationships impossible. She had lied about her drinking and had a pattern of binge drinking from early adolescence but had never done anything about it. She thought of herself as a tough-minded woman who had lapses, only this relapse wasn't going away. She promised to "hunker down" and get to work, and she did. On her seventieth birthday, she passed six months of sobriety and had her cart privileges returned. With the counselor's recommendation, she also got her driver's license back. She has joined a real estate firm selling resales in the retirement community and is busier than ever. And she has found a man her age whom she considers her best friend and companion. In the time she has available after work, they take advantage of the many cultural events in the community. During the hottest months of the summer, they go to the mountains. Little happens at work during those months and if someone contacts the agency she can handle it on the Internet and by phone.

Wanda's counselor told me, "I'm never surprised when people tell me that they have a history of drinking even though they deny it early in treatment. I wonder about late-onset alcoholism and, while I'm sure it exists, many older people with no actual history of drinking problems find alcohol aversive both in taste and in its effect. I think Wanda is one of many tough-minded successful women in our society who fill their lives so full that when they take a break and try and relax, many emotional issues come up they'd rather not deal with. So they work hard, have lots of acquaintances, and stay very busy. When they retire, many years of denial and ignoring problems begin to have an impact. The fact that Wanda read the articles I suggested and came prepared to discuss them gave her a large body of information. When she was ready to begin changing, the material she read came in very handy.

"I don't want to define Wanda as a success story. Alcohol isn't her only problem. When she becomes too tired to work or fill up her time with other activities, it wouldn't surprise me if she had a relapse. Right now, she's had a scare and she's very motivated. I've referred her for counseling to help her understand the impact of her early life, but she's put it off. I suspect she's had some very bad traumas and maybe she can avoid discussing them but I think sooner or later they'll come back to haunt her."

SUMMARY

This chapter deals with the serious problem of substance abuse among older men and women. A number of physical problems have their origins in heavy alcohol use, but physicians often neglect to find out about drinking and therefore treat the physical problem and not the underlying problem of alcohol abuse. The chapter discusses treatment issues with substance abuse including brief treatment, natural healing, and self-help groups. A case study describes an older retired woman experiencing serious alcohol problems and the counseling she receives to control her drinking after suffering from a serious alcohol-related accident.

USEFUL WEB SITES

About.com (2008). "Alcoholism and Pain Killer Abuse Increasing among Older Adults." http://alcoholism.about.com/od/prescription/a/older _pain.htm.

Alcohol Abuse Screening Quiz (2008). http://alcoholism.about.com/od/ problem/a/blquiz1.htm.

Joseph Gfroerer, Michael Penne, Michael Pemberton, and Ralph Folsom (2003). "Substance Abuse Treatment Need among Older Adults in 2020: The Impact of the Aging Baby-boom Cohort." *Drug and Alcohol Dependence* 69: 127–135. https://medicine.johnstrogerhospital.org/cru/ images/education/519cd99e959493c0c6ad6bf40b928794.pdf.

Medicinenet.com (2008). Alcoholism. http://www.medicinenet.com/alcohol _abuse_and_alcoholism/article.htm.

National Council on Drug Dependence (2008). Substance abuse symptom checklist. http://www.ncadd-sfv.org/symptoms/symptom_checklist .html.

REFERENCES

Adams, W. L., Barry, K. L., and Fleming, M. F. (1996). "Screening for Problem Drinking in Older Primary Care Patients." *Journal of the American Medical Association* 276 (24).

Atkinson, R. (1995). "Treatment Programs for Aging Alcoholics." In Beresford, T., and Gomberg, E., *Alcohol and Aging.* New York: Oxford University Press: 186–210.

Babor, T. F., and Higgins-Biddle, J. C. (May 2000). "Alcohol Screening and Brief Intervention: Dissemination Strategies for Medical Practice and Public Health." *Addiction* 95 (5): 677–87.

Barrick, C., and Connors, G. J. (2002). "Relapse Prevention and Maintaining Abstinence in Older Adults with Alcohol-use Disorders. *Drugs and Aging* 19: 583–94.

Bien, T. J., Miller, W. R., and Tonigan, J. S. (1993). "Brief Interventions for Alcohol Problems: A Review." *Addictions* 88 (3): 315–35.

Biernacki, P. (1986). *Pathways from Heroin Addiction: Recover Without Treatment.* Philadelphia: Temple University Press.

Bisson, J., Nadeau, L., and Demers, A. (May 1999). "The Validity of the CAGE Scale to Screen Heavy Drinking and Drinking Problems in a General Population." *Addiction* 94 (5): 715–23.

Blow, F. C. (2007). "Substance Abuse among Older Adults: Treatment Improvement Protocol (TIP) Series 26." Substance Abuse and Mental Health Services Administration. Retrieved November 17, 2007 from: http://ncadi.samhsa.gov/govpubs/BKD250/.

Burge, S. K., Amodei, N., Elkin, B., Catala, S., Andrew, S. R., Lane, P. A., and Seale, J. P. (1997). "An Evaluation of Two Primary Care Interventions for Alcohol Abuse among Mexican-American Patients." *Addiction* 92 (12): 1705–16.

Chang, G., Wilkins-Haug, L., Berman, S., and Goetz, M. A. (1999). "Brief Intervention for Alcohol Use in Pregnancy: A Randomized Trial." *Addiction* 94 (10): 1499–1508.

Fleming, M. F., Barry, K. L., Manwell, L. B., Johnson, K., and London, R. (1997). "Brief Physician Advice for Problem Alcohol Drinkers: A Randomized Controlled Trial in Community-based Primary Care Practices." *Journal of the American Medical Association* 277 (13): 1039–45.

Fleming, M., and Manwell, L. B. (1998). "Brief Intervention in Primary Care Settings: A Primary Treatment Method for At-risk, Problem, and Dependent Drinkers." *Alcohol Research and Health* 23 (2): 128–37.

Gentilello, L. M., Donovan, D. M., Dunn, C. W., and Rivara, F. P. (1995). "Alcohol Interventions in Trauma Centers: Current Practice and Future Directions." *Journal of the American Medical Association* 274 (13): 1043–48.

Granfield, R., and Cloud, W. (Winter 1996). "The Elephant That No One Sees: Natural Recovery among Middle-class Addicts. *Journal of Drug Issues* 26: 45–61.

Herman, M. (2000). "Psychotherapy with Substance Abusers: Integration of Psychodynamic and Cognitive-behavioral Approaches." *American Journal of Psychotherapy* 54 (4): 574–79.

Higgins-Biddle, J. C., Babor, T. F., Mullahy, J., Daniels, J., and Mcree, B. (1997). "Alcohol Screening and Brief Interventions: Where Research Meets Practice." *Connecticut Medicine* 61: 565–75.

Hingson, R., Scotch, N., Day, N., and Culbert, A. (1980). "Recognizing and Seeking Help for Drinking Problems." *Journal of Studies on Alcohol* 41: 1102–17.

Humphreys, K. (Winter 1998). "Can Addiction-Related Self-help/Mutual Aid Groups Lower Demand for Professional Substance Abuse Treatment?" *Social Policy* 29 (2): 13–17.

Liberto, J. G., and Oslin, D. W. (1995). "Early Versus Late Onset of Alcoholism in the Elderly." *International Journal of Addiction* 30 (13–14): 1799–1818.

Menninger, J. A. (Spring 2002). "Source Assessment and Treatment of Alcoholism and Substance-related Disorders in the Elderly." *Bulletin of the Menninger Clinic* 66 (2): 166–184A.

Miller, W. R., and Rollnick, S. (1991). *Motivational Interviewing: Preparing People for Change*. New York: Guilford Press.

Miller, W. R., and Sanchez, V. C. (1994). "Motivating Young Adults for Treatment and Lifestyle Change." In Howard, G. S., and Nathan, P. E. (eds.), *Alcohol Use and Misuse by Young Adults*. Notre Dame, IN: University of Notre Dame Press: 55–81.

Mukamal, K. J., Mittleman, M. A., Longstreth, W. T., Newman, A. B., Fried, L. P., and Siscovick, D. S. (2004). "Self-reports of Alcohol Consumption and Falls in Older Adults: Cross-sectional and Longitudinal Analyses of the Cardiovascular Health Study." *Journal of the American Geriatrics Society* 52: 1174–79.

National Institute for Alcohol Abuse and Alcoholism, Department of Health and Human Services, Alcohol and Health (1997). *Ninth Special Report to the United States on Alcohol and Health* (NIH Publication No. 97-4017). Washington, D.C.: U.S. Government Printing Office.

Onder, G., Landi, E., Delia Vedova, C., Atkinson, H., Pedone, C., Cesari, M., et al. (2002). "Moderate Alcohol Consumption and Adverse Drug Reactions among Older Adults." *Pharmacoepidemiological Drug Safety* 11: 385–92.

Oslin, D. W. (2004). "Late-life Alcoholism: Issues Relevant to the Geriatric Psychiatrist." *American Journal of Geriatric Psychiatry* 12: 571–83.

Peele, S. (1989). *The Diseasing of America: Addiction Treatment Out of Control*. Lexington, MA: Lexington Books.

Roizen, R., Calahan, D., Lambert, E., Wiebel, W., and Shanks, P. (1978). "Spontaneous Remission among Untreated Problem Drinkers." In Kandel, D. (ed.), *Longitudinal Research on Drug Use*. Washington, D.C.: Hemisphere Publishing.

Seligman, M. E. P. (1995). "The Effectiveness of Psychotherapy: The Consumer Reports Study." *American Psychologist* 50 (12): 965–74.

Snow, M. (1973). "Maturing Out of Narcotic Addiction in New York City." *International Journal of the Addictions* 8 (6): 932–38.

Sobell, L., Sobell, M., Toneatto, T., and Leo, G. (1993). "What Triggers the Resolution of Alcohol Problems Without Treatment?" *Alcoholism: Clinical and Experimental Research* 17 (2): 217–24.

Stall, R., and Biernacki, P. (1989). "Spontaneous Remission from the Problematic Use of Substances." *International Journal of the Addictions* 21: 1–23.

Stewart, K. B., and Richards, A. B. (2000). "Recognizing and Managing your Patient's Alcohol Abuse." *Nursing* 30 (2): 56–60.

Substance Abuse and Mental Health Services Administration (SAMHSA) (1998). *Substance Abuse among Older Adults: Treatment Improvement Protocol* (TIP; Series #26). Rockville, MD: U.S. Department of Health and Human Services.

Trice, H., and Roman, P. (1970). "Delabeling, Relabeling, and Alcoholics Anonymous." *Social Problems* 17: 538–46.

Waldorf, D., Reinarman, C., and Murphy, S. (1991). *Cocaine Changes: The Experience of Using and Quitting*. Philadelphia: Temple University Press.

Winick, C. (1962). "Maturing Out of Narcotic Addiction." *Bulletin on Narcotics* 6 (1).

CHAPTER 16

Dangerous People: Men and Women Who Are Physically and Emotionally Abusive

I don't want to end this book without discussing abusive relationships. Age doesn't make the men and women who are verbally and physically abusive earlier in life any less abusive. It would be nice to think so, but if you are about to become involved with someone and you've begun to notice little signs that people you've begun to date have short fuses; seem excessively controlling, jealous, and angry; or abuse substances, you'd better believe that it won't be long before you experience abusive behavior. It may not be of the sort where violence is involved, but verbal abuse can be very hurtful and emotionally damaging. My advice is to find out about people's past and why prior relationships failed. If abuse was involved don't be a social worker and think that you can cure it with your caring and warm-hearted treatment. Abuse is a deep-seated problem and whether someone is 20 or 65, it's damaging to the body and the spirit.

WHAT WE KNOW ABOUT ABUSIVE PEOPLE

We know a lot about abusive people. We know that they often tend to have been abused as children. They can be pathologically jealous and have low opinions of people of the opposite sex. And they have a tendency to deny the pain they cause. When confronted by the damage they've inflicted on others, they deny that it ever happened or somehow believe that the other person is to blame.

We know that many abusive people have a limited ability to express feelings and often use violence to convey the dark emotions building up inside. And we know that abuse is more likely to occur when people drink or use drugs.

Abusive people believe that lovers and mates are very likely to be unfaithful, a belief that is used continually to justify the pain they inflict. We know that men and women who have both been abused as children often come together in relationships so violent that it is difficult to explain the damage they do. In some bizarre way, abuse becomes a way of expressing love for many of these couples.

DESCRIBING ABUSERS

The following comes from a book by the author (Glicken 2005) on relationship problems between men and women and contains information about abusive relationships:

- Many abusive males have, themselves, been physically abused by parents, caretakers, or other family members. The physical abuse frequently includes sexual abuse. Data would suggest that roughly 65 percent of the men who abuse women and children have themselves been abused.

- While it might seem odd that an abused child would grow up to abuse others because the experience would, hopefully, have sensitized him to the dreadful ramifications of abuse, the dynamics are such that unconscious rage often directs the behavior. One client of mine told me that he was so angry that every encounter with another human being left him throttling an impulse to "Hurt somebody real bad. I never knew why I was so mad all the time but I was and somebody was going to pay for it, that was for sure."

- This need for payback is often reinforced by other people in the abuser's life who believe that physical abuse is the best way to keep those we love "in line." In truth, an abuser may believe that his abusive behavior is far too mild because important people in his life ridicule him for being too meek.

- Abusive people are frequently insensitive to the pain they inflict. When one asks them about an abusive episode, they understate the harm done. They deny hearing bones break or believe that the victim is the responsible one since he or she should not have been sitting the way he or she was when they were struck. Or the abuser will tell you that the victim should have seen that the abuser was angry and removed himself or herself from the situation.

- Many abusers believe that victims like to be abused and, therefore, they are only fulfilling the wishes of the victim. When x-rays are produced which indicate that harm has been done, all too many abusers will argue that the victim had a congenital weakness in the area damaged or that they were not struck that hard.
- Abusers are often pathologically suspicious and jealous and see infidelity everywhere.

Some writers believe that abusers are so incapable of intimacy that distrust of the motives of lovers and mates is translated into fear of love, affection, and intimacy. To allow someone to love you is to invite terrible psychic pain. To avoid the inevitability of such pain, abuse is a way of negating others. Ridicule and emotional abuse go hand in hand with the physical abuse. Abused women are often encouraged to be as physically unattractive as possible. When women fail to comply with the need to minimize attractiveness, the abuser may make certain that his abuse helps to accomplish this through physical beatings.

Many abusers report that they have affairs as preemptive strikes to guarantee their emotional safety when wives or girlfriends "inevitably" become unfaithful. The abusers belief in the inevitability of infidelity even when loved ones become so emotionally and physically scarred that they no longer have the emotional strength to seek out other relationships. The more a lover or spouse becomes unattractive, the more the abuser ridicules his or her looks to further discourage seeking other relationships.

A great deal of abusive behavior comes in the midst of substance abuse. Substances not only give abusive people the courage to abuse, but they permit the release of repressed rage. For the victim of abuse, the abuser may appear irrational in his outbursts. However, often the abuser is more in touch with the abuse he or she suffered as a child under the influence of alcohol or drugs. This may not be a conscious memory as much as a reminder of feelings of powerlessness and rage. Abusive people who use substances are at their most dangerous when they are intoxicated or high. Not only are they less able to control their rage, but they are operating in states of altered consciousness in which prior abuse to them creates feelings of powerlessness that strengthen rage reactions. The wife of an abusive client told me, "He could be the most charming man who ever lived when he was sober, but get a drink in him and look out. He'd kick the dog, then he'd beat on me and then, if the kids were around, he'd whack them pretty good as well. Something happened to him when he drank. It was like he changed personalities. He was a monster, really. Just an awful, abusive, crazed monster when he drank."

Abusive people often have difficulty using language to convey emotions, desires, and expectations. When victims do not do as abusers desire, hitting or ridicule are the ways abusers have been taught to deal with anger since they also distrust language. For them, words are signs of weakness. When they *do* use language that conveys feeling, the experience makes them feel oddly powerless. Language that causes emotional harm to others is perfectly OK to the abuser, and many abuse victims say that the worst thing about the abuse is the terrible things said to them by the abuser. Not surprisingly, abusive people may be seen as mild-mannered and calm elsewhere, reverting to abuse and tyranny only in the safety of their homes.

Many writers report that abusers feel remorse after an episode of abuse. The term "Honeymoon Period" is used to define the remorseful period in which, out of guilt, the abuser becomes warm, loving, and tender. Abuse victims describe this period as the time when their lives are the happiest. As with other reinforcements, the victim is addicted to these moments and may put up with continued abuse because it often results in a short period during which the relationship is at its best. Some abusers suggest that these periods are short-lived because victims encourage additional abuse so that they can move back into the honeymoon period. While this may occasionally be true, it is more likely that the rage inside abusive people has a limited period in which it can lie dormant before outbursts of anger take place again.

PERSONAL STORY: AN OLDER ADULT ABUSIVE RELATIONSHIP

"I was 63 when I met Robert. He was a successful real estate agent and a very charming and attractive man a few years older than me. When we first began dating he couldn't have been nicer. He had a sort of old world courtesy and respect for me that I found really wonderful and very different from the men I'd been dating. I noticed early on that he drank a lot but he seemed to be able to hold his liquor and I didn't notice that it affected him much. That changed after we began what I thought was a committed relationship.

"The first thing I noticed were small put-downs. He'd mention that he didn't like what I was wearing but then he'd apologize and say that my outfit was perfectly fine. Or he'd make snide comments about my friends and ask in a condescending way what I could possibly see in them. He'd make unflattering remarks about my body and then say that my body was wonderful. I found it increasingly hurtful and told him so. He'd always apologize. I also noticed that the longer we dated the more I began to feel that he was seeing other people. He'd cancel dates at the last minute or come up with excuses why he couldn't see me that seemed lame, to say the least.

"One day he screamed at me over some slight and I told him I'd had quite enough and walked out of a restaurant where we were having dinner. He sent roses and called to apologize and finally I relented and saw him. He promised never to do that again and blamed it on his business and a bad real estate market that was driving a lot of real estate people out of work. I readily agreed that he had reason to feel stressed but told him I wouldn't take another outburst. He promised it would never happen again but it did. This time I told him we were done for good and not to call me again. He did, of course, and started showing up at places where he shouldn't have. I begun to suspect he was stalking me. He denied it but I knew he was.

"I decided to check him out, something I should have done earlier. I found out that he had a history of abusive behavior dating back to the first of four marriages, all of which went bad because of his abusive behavior. One wife called the police when he beat her up and he was sent to jail for six months.

"I've never been with a man who was abusive but after my experience with Robert I would caution women to check carefully on the people they date, and when signs of violence or abuse pop up, to immediately get out of the relationship. I had to go to court and get a restraining order and threaten to inform his employer of his abusive behavior before he stopped. One of my friends saw him with another woman recently. I wonder if he's doing the same thing to her that he did with me. If so I hope she has the emotional strength to get out of it. I started worrying about my safety. At 64, that's a pretty awful thing to have hanging over you when you should be enjoying life and not worrying about your safety."—G. H.

FINAL WORDS

If you are in an abusive relationship, you need to seek professional help as quickly as possible. Sometimes that help includes withdrawing from the abuser. Other times that help may include reporting the abuse to the police and having the abuser enter mandatory treatment or face a jail sentence. Don't let anyone abuse you. It will lead to emotional damage, physical and health problems, and in too many cases, permanent disfigurement and even death.

REFERENCE

Glicken, M. D. (2005). *Ending the Sex Wars: A Woman's Guide to Understanding Men*. Lincoln, NE: iUniverse.

CHAPTER 17

The Road Less Traveled: Making the Most of Love, Family, and Friends

In this book on relationships I've tried to prepare you for the often very satisfying world of older adult love, romance, and intimacy, a world that offers a great deal of independence to take the road you've wanted to take during your working and parenting time. I call it the "road less traveled" because it offers you so much opportunity to do many of the things you weren't able to do earlier in your life. Perhaps another way to say this is "achieving your dreams."

If you've been unlucky in love and long for the right person, or what Jewish people call "your *beshert*" (your chosen one), then this is the time to start looking for that person. But you have to put aside your prejudices and look in places you may not have looked before because of your own personal biases. Places of worship are better places to meet singles than clubs or bars. Do you only want to date women or men who are 20 years younger than you? Good luck, because your population of eligible singles will be very small. Do you think that only educated people are worth dating? There are wonderful people out there who are smart, funny, and sensitive, but who may not have been able to go to college for a number of practical reasons—but they read, and think, and long for love, just like you do.

Pessimism is everything it's cracked up to be. If you want to look at things negatively and assume that nothing will work, chances are that they won't. Self-fulfilling prophecies usually turn out as we expected them to. You can as easily be optimistic and recognize that you have plenty of time to test the waters, but if you take a chance and it doesn't work out, take it again until it does work out.

This isn't pop psychology or psychobabble. There is considerable research to show that people who are optimistic live longer, handle stress better, are physically healthier, and are much more satisfied with life. The road less traveled takes courage and perseverance. It also means changing some negative and pesky attitudes and beliefs.

I think America needs its older people. There is work to be done in our government, in our charitable organizations, in our places of worship, in our schools, and in every avenue of American life. I think you should take part in helping our country out during this time of national difficulty. You can do it by mentoring children who are taking a wrong turn in life and offering support to older people with few resources or friends. You can use your expertise to help others and to help make our country work as it should. Our democracy is based on the notion of a citizen government, not one run by a political class or by bureaucrats but by us.

No one ever said that older people should tune out of life and just play golf and cards for the next 30 years. You have a long life ahead of you. Make the most of it. I have a core of friends in their seventies and eighties who play tennis. One is on the board of Sun City Phoenix. Another continues to build houses. Another continues to run a successful insurance company, and yet another is on the city council and drives for Meals on Wheels. I don't know of anyone who's retired who doesn't take an active role in the civic and charitable life of our community. Many have had heart problems but they continue to be active. Some have battled cancer but they're out on the tennis court and in the community most days. These are the ordinary older people of America, and they continue to live rich lives full of activity and energy.

Having good friends who are positive in the way they view life is vital to happiness in retirement. If you have people around you who always focus on the negatives or tell you why you can't follow the road less traveled, you need to make adjustments in how much time you spend with them, what you talk to them about, and how seriously you take them. Most of us can "tune out" things we don't want to hear. You can do it too with friends and family who are negative and intrude on your dreams.

I have a friend who was president of a large community college and wanted to go to the magical city of Machu Picchu in the Peruvian Andes. During her trip she was riding a horse that bucked her off and she broke her femur. For the next couple of days she was driven along back roads on an old bus and had people she didn't know minister to her pain until she finally had surgery in Lima, Peru and then flew home to the United States. She endured several additional surgeries. Would she do it again? Absolutely! Why? Because it was a dream and she felt compelled to follow it. When she talks about her trip she almost never mentions the accident, but instead her eyes mist over as she talks about the Andes, the wonderful people she met, how she saw Machu Picchu in the mist, and as the mist lifted, how she saw the most marvelous sight she had ever seen. Did she have people telling her how crazy it was to ride horses in the Andes? By the droves. Did she care? Not a bit. She had seen a sight that would never leave her and she'd had experiences one thinks about forever. At age 70, that's saying a lot.

The economy will have a great deal to do with how you approach retirement. I'm optimistic about the health of the economy, but I'm concerned that not enough people approaching retirement have saved enough or have planned early enough for their financial futures. I think increasing energy and food costs are likely to be part of the overall picture in America for some time to come. It's vital that you spend time with people who understand finances, work out a financial game plan, and stick with it. Many of us only begin to recognize the need for wise financial advice later in life. Perhaps that's because we are more aware of retirement and are more settled financially and emotionally to do what needs to be done to have a secure retirement. In any event, saving, wise advice, and a financial game plan are especially important in an era of increasing costs and decreasing pension plans.

Our extended families offer us the opportunity for a great deal of joy. Who among us doesn't become emotional at the thought of our adult children marrying or the birth of a grandchild? Because we are wiser now, we have the chance to make a real impact on the health of our extended families and to be the people of wisdom who mentor the children of our children.

Finally, the road less traveled is an opportunity for you to broaden your horizons intellectually. There are many adult-learning programs at local colleges and universities. For those of you who want to go on and get a degree or a different degree from the one you have now, many universities and colleges offer reduced tuition to older adults. Education in America is one of the great bargains. It's inexpensive and it's good. Take the opportunity to broaden your intellectual horizons. Keeping your mind active intellectually is one of the best ways I know of to stay healthy. Too many older adults lock themselves into rigid mindsets of not wanting to know other sides of arguments or new ways of thinking. "I'm too old and too set in my ways to learn anything new or change my opinions" is just another way of saying "I don't want to because it makes me work a little." Intellectually rigid people do badly when crises hit because they are ill prepared to handle new situations and new conditions. This goes for all of us, even those of us who have advanced degrees. Learning for the sake of learning is stimulating. and knowledge, for certain, is power.

A therapist I know recently told me about an older female who spoke endlessly about the move toward "socialism" and the government's intrusion in our lives. In her view we shouldn't pay taxes, help others, concern ourselves with the community, or do anything most of us think of as positive behavior. The therapist told me she was so full of bile and hatred that therapy went nowhere. Her negative view of the responsibilities of citizenship reduced her ability to think in a positive and optimistic way.

My friend Peter came to Prescott less than a year ago and yet he is involved in a program called Boys to Men, a mentoring program for boys without male role models in their lives. Today, while having coffee, he called me over to meet some of the people he works with in the program and before I knew it, I was agreeing to help them out. There are people who shine with optimism. They should be your role models because their optimism and positive view of the world lead to better health and longer life.

I want to take this opportunity to thank you for reading my book. I hope it's helped you gain confidence to meet the challenges of love, romance, and intimacy and reap the rewards of life as an older adult. I plan to offer interactive and on-site seminars on older adult love, romance, and intimacy. You can find out more about my seminars by going to http://www.morleyglicken.com. I look forward to meeting you online and in person. Thanks again, and best wishes for the future.

Dr. Morley D. Glicken

PERSONAL STORY: FINDING LOVE AT 70

"My husband died of a heart attack five years ago when I was 65. We had a good relationship. Up until his death he had been a healthy and vigorous man. We thought we would be together until we were 90—maybe longer. It was tough at first to deal with being single. I felt lonely and anxious about going out by myself. Luckily, I had a core of good friends who were also single and we did a lot of social things together. Still, I missed having a man in my life.

"I dated a few people but no one really seemed to be what I was looking for. What was I looking for? I guess someone with a lot of the good qualities of my husband without some of the bad ones. For all his good qualities he had a temper. and he could be very dismissive of people who didn't agree with him, including me. And he could be very bossy at times. What I liked was his optimism and 'can do' spirit. He hiked and loved the outdoors. He wasn't much for symphonies and theater and, much as I encouraged him to go with me, he'd often fall asleep or just look bored. I usually went with girl friends rather than deal with his attitude toward the things I loved.

"I met a man about a year ago. He liked many of the things I did and slowly and over time, we started dating. It felt seamless and easy being with him. And he was a gentleman and knew how to treat a lady. In time, as we dated and became intimate, we fell in love. Rockets didn't go off and trumpets didn't blast every time we were together, but we enjoyed one another's company and felt at ease with each other. I had a medical problem while we were dating and he was there for me, helping me get to doctor's appointments and being with me when I felt down. And I could talk to him about anything. He seemed happy to listen. If I needed advice, he'd give it to me. He was always very easy with his advice and never made me feel as if he was intruding.

"He began to stay over at my house, and it felt good. We fell into an easy and relaxed relationship. He's very good with money and helped me make some investments which turned out well even during these bad economic times. He never acted superior or made me feel dumb the way my husband sometimes made me feel. He has two wonderful children who adore him. We do things together a lot. It's the sort of close family I always dreamed of but never had when I was married. My kids moved away soon after they finished college and we've not been as close as I'd hoped we'd be. Having John's family has given me the sense of a larger support group I never had before.

"We never went through infatuation or had a strong need for sex. When it happened it was very good, but we didn't rush into it and he seemed content to let our relationship build before we did anything physical. He sold his house and now we live together in my house. He pays half of the expenses, which has been a financial relief for me. We find happiness in all sorts of ways. We've begun bird-watching and joined an archeology group to explore Native American sites in the Southwest, something we're both passionate about, and we take advantage of the many free social and cultural events in town. His friends have become mine and mine have become his. We're a couple, and believe me, that's a wonderful feeling. Being with someone at my age is like having a second chance at life.

"John and I met at a block party in my neighborhood. We sat and talked for a long time. I felt that he was a very nice person but the bells didn't ring. When he called me a few days later to ask me out for coffee, we talked about books, and films, and the outdoors. It was the most relaxed date I've ever been on.

"Pretty soon we were going to see movies and plays together. It all happened slowly and, over time, we could both see that we liked each other. Like my husband, his wife had died after a long and painful illness. He felt guilty about dating and so did I. You live with someone for 35 years and it's not easy to push them out of your mind or forget the wonderful times you had together.

"I think the slow and easy way our relationship developed is what made it work, and I tell my single friends that infatuation is for young people. For us, a gentle and easy relationship that develops and grows over time, maybe like a fine wine, is what works best. All I can say is that I'm happier than I've ever been in my life, and if the insurance people are right and we have 20 more years to live—or maybe even more—then I guess I'll have almost as long with John as I had with my husband. It's a wonderful feeling."—L. S.

Index

About the Author

Dr. Morley D. Glicken is the former Dean of the Worden School of Social Service in San Antonio; the founding Director of the Master of Social Work Department at California State University, San Bernardino; the past Director of the Master of Social Work Program at the University of Alabama; and the former Executive Director of Jewish Family Service of Greater Tucson. He has also held faculty positions in social work at the University of Kansas and Arizona State University. He currently teaches in the Department of Social Work at Arizona State University in Tempe, Arizona and is the Executive Director of the Institute for Positive Growth, a research and training cooperative in Prescott, Arizona.

Dr. Glicken received his BA degree in social work with a minor in psychology from the University of North Dakota and holds a Master of Social Work degree from the University of Washington and the Master of Public Administration and Doctor of Social Work degrees from the University of Utah. He is a member of Phi Kappa Phi Honorary Fraternity.

In 2010, Praeger/ABC-CLIO will publish his book *Retirement for Workaholics: Life After Work in a Downsized Economy*. In 2009, Praeger/ABC-CLIO published his book *A Simple Guide to Retirement* (with Brian Haas). Elsevier, Inc. published his books *Evidence-Based Practice with Troubled Children and Adolescents: A Psychosocial Perspective* and *Evidence-Based Counseling and Psychotherapy with an Aging Population*, also in 2009. In 2008 he published *A Guide to Writing for Human*

Service Professionals for Rowman and Littlefield Publishers. In 2006 he published *Life Lessons from Resilient People*, published by Sage Publications. He published *Working with Troubled Men: A Practitioner's Guide* for Lawrence Erlbaum Publishers in 2005 and *Improving the Effectiveness of the Helping Professions: An Evidence-Based Approach to Practice* in 2004 for Sage Publications. In 2003 he published *Violent Young Children* and *Understanding and Using the Strengths Perspective* for Allyn and Bacon/Longman Publishers. Dr. Glicken published two books for Allyn and Bacon/Longman Publishers in 2002: *The Role of the Helping Professions in the Treatment of Victims and Perpetrators of Crime* (with Dale Sechrest) and *A Simple Guide to Social Research*.

Dr. Glicken has published over 50 articles in professional journals and has written extensively on personnel issues for Dow Jones, the publisher of the *Wall Street Journal*. He has held clinical social work licenses in Alabama and Kansas and is a member of the Academy of Certified Social Workers. He is currently Professor Emeritus in Social Work at California State University, San Bernardino and Executive Director of the Institute for Personal Growth: A Research, Treatment, and Training Institute in Prescott, Arizona offering consulting services in counseling, research, and management.

More information about Dr. Glicken may be obtained on his Web site: www.morleyglicken.com. A listing of all of his books may be found on Amazon.com at: https://authorcentral.amazon.com/v/1973805540. He may be contacted at: mglicken@msn.com.